GW00732535

Crochet Things

Also by
Rae Compton and Michael Harvey
in Piccolo

Knitting Things

Rae Compton and Michael Harvey

Crochet Things

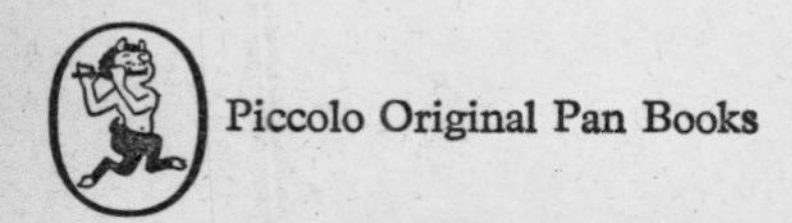

We gratefully acknowledge the help provided by Patons and Baldwins Ltd for their check crochet.

First published 1978 by Pan Books Ltd,
Cavaye Place, London SW10 9PG
© Rae Compton & Michael Harvey 1978
ISBN 0 330 25526 6
Made and printed in Great Britain by
Cox & Wyman Ltd, London, Reading and Fakenham
This book is sold subject to the condition that it shall not, by way of trade or otherwise, be lent, re-sold, hired out or otherwise circulated without the publisher's prior consent in any form of binding or cover other than that in which it is published and without a similar condition including this condition being imposed on the subsequent purchaser

Contents

1 Preparing things

It's great fun to be able to crochet so let's get down to work and learn as quickly as possible.

A ball of yarn and a crochet hook are all you really need to start with, but there are one or two other things that it is best to mention right at the beginning.

Have somewhere special to keep your crochet things. A clean polythene bag will do until you can crochet yourself a workbag.

Things you will need

Here is a list of things to keep in your workbag. Tick them as you collect them – and don't forget to put them back in the bag each time you use them, so that they are always easily found.

Balls of yarn (Patons Double Knitting Wool or Patons Trident Double Knitting Wool are both suitable for learners)
Crochet hooks (this book uses only sizes 4.00 mm; 4.50 mm; 5.00 mm; and 6.00 mm)
Small pair of sharp scissors
Blunt-pointed wool needle
Ruler
Box of rustless pins

Why do you need these things?

Here are the answers.

Balls of yarn

Yarn is the name given to everything that you can crochet. It may be linen, silk, cotton, or wool (all natural fibres) or nylon, courtelle, acrilan or polyester (all man-made fibres) or it might even be string! But when you are just beginning you will find it much easier to use wool or wool mixed with a man-made fibre, for it is softer and stretches more easily than man-made fibres.

There will be plenty of time to try out all the other yarns once you know what the stitches are like and feel that you can really crochet.

Be careful that you don't call nylon and other man-made fibres 'wool'. A great many people do make this mistake just because man-made yarns are used for knitting and crochet. Be certain that you know the difference between the various types of yarns.

Buy a new ball of wool so that you can learn easily and don't try to learn with scraps of yarn that may have even been used before. If you do, it may be difficult to see how the stitches are made, or even where to put the hook next.

Either Patons Double Knitting Wool or Patons Trident Double Knitting Wool are suitable for beginners. You can go on to using scraps when you have managed to make most of the things in this book.

Choose a colour that you like and one that is not too dark or too light. The mid-shades will let you see exactly what you are doing, where the dark ones make it more difficult and the very light ones soil more easily.

Crochet hooks

Once crochet hooks were made of bone and very special ones were even made of ivory. Today they are usually made of anodized aluminium or plastic with only the very fine ones, used for lacy work, being made in steel.

Well-designed hooks are easy to work with. They are made by firms like Abel Morrall and Milward's and come in a range of 16 different sizes.

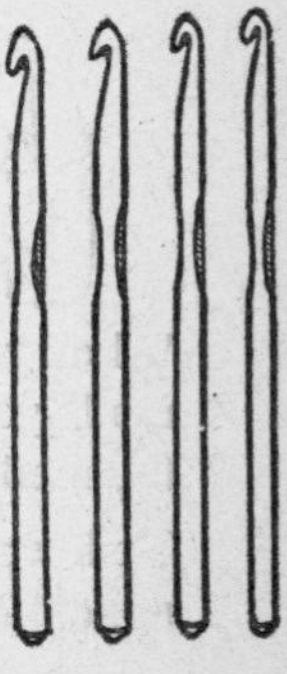

It is not long since crochet hook sizes were altered to metric sizing. We have kept to metric sizes in this book, but if you use pre-metric instructions you will need to know the metric equivalent of the old size. Here is a table which gives the metric equivalent of each of the old numbered sizes from thinnest to thickest.

Table of crochet hook sizes

metric size (mm)	*before metrication (number)*	
0.60	6	
0.75	5	
1.00	4	
1.25	3	steel
1.50	2.5	
1.75	2	
2.00	14	
2.50	12	
3.00	11	
3.50	9	
4.00	8	
4.50	7	aluminium or plastic
5.00	6	
5.50	5	
6.00	4	
7.00	2	

Scissors

It is better to cut yarn than to break it, so always have a small pair of sharp-pointed scissors ready. Wool that has nylon mixed with it will be very difficult to break and if you don't cut it you may hurt your fingers.

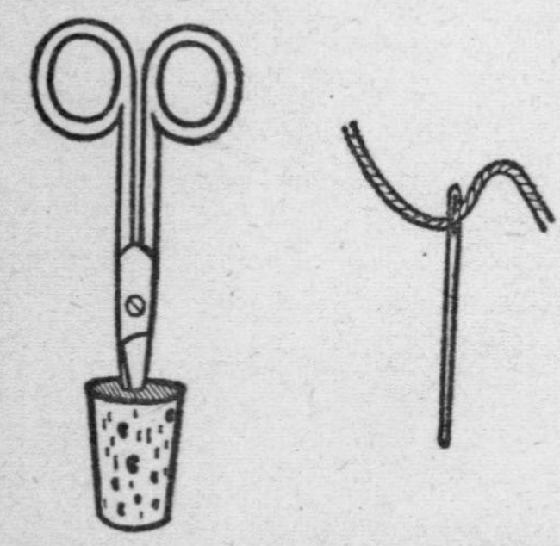

When you are ready to finish off and sew up the things you have made you will need scissors to cut off the ends of yarn to make the finished article neat and tidy.

To keep the points of the scissors from spoiling your workbag poke them into a cork and then you won't stab them into yourself by mistake.

Ruler

It is most important to get into the habit of always measuring your crochet on a flat surface using a ruler. A measuring tape is

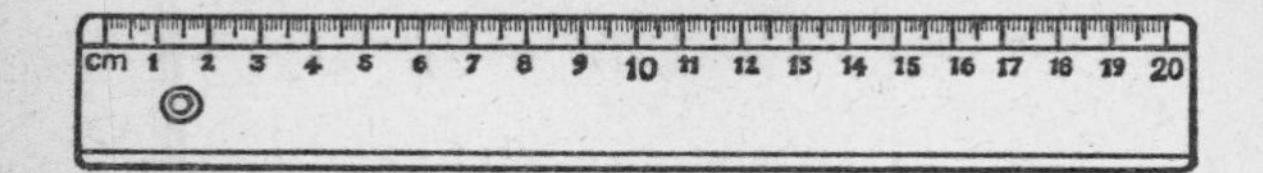

not so good because it can stretch. A tape may also tempt you to measure the work on your knee or on the arm of your chair. Neither is likely to be a flat surface and so the measurement may not be accurate.

All the measurements given in this book are in centimetres, so a ruler which is marked clearly in centimetres is necessary.

Wool needle

A wool needle, which is sometimes called a knitter's needle, is the best type to use for sewing up the things you make and for darning in the ends of yarn.

It is easy to thread for it has a large eye but what is more important is that it does not split the strands of yarn and make untidy seams.

Pins

When you have finished crocheting and are ready to make up things, you will need pins to keep the pieces of crochet flat while

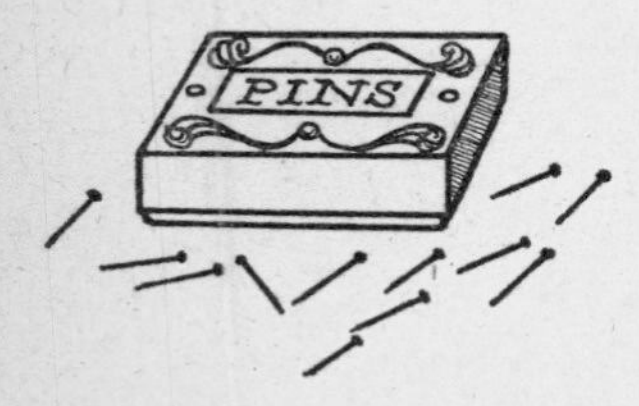

you press them, and you will also need pins to keep the pieces together while you sew them in place.

Rustless pins will last for a long time and will also never spoil your work.

About this book

The quickest way to being able to crochet is to work, step by step, through this book.

After each step there is something for you to make so that you can practise what you have just learnt. It really helps to do this because you can manage the next step more easily.

Once you have mastered each step then all the things in the last chapter can be made without any problems.

If you start anywhere just because one of the designs is exactly what you want, you may find that you don't know enough to complete it, or you may get into a muddle and have to spend a long time getting it right.

Soon you will be making things for yourself and your friends, things to wear or to decorate your room with, to make as presents for your family or even to help raise funds for charity at a fête or sale of work.

Whether you can knit or not you will also find our companion book *Knitting Things* handy to keep in your work basket. Its chapter on 'Sewing Things Up', which clearly shows you how to make pompons, fringing, tassels, and so on which can be used as trims for your crocket work, will be especially useful to readers of *Crochet Things*.

2 Beginning things

All crochet begins with making a slip loop, so let's practise that first.

Fold the end of the yarn over itself to form a loop.

Hold the loop between the thumb and fingers of your left hand.

Using your right hand, draw another loop of yarn from further along nearer the ball through the first loop.

Draw it up to form a loop that won't come loose when you let go of it.

Using Patons Double Knitting Wool or Patons Trident Double Knitting Wool, make a loop in this way and then slip it on to a size 4.50 crochet hook.

Draw the loop up so that it is not loose but sits neatly and firmly immediately behind the hooked part of the hook. The rest of the hook is called the shank.

Crochet is worked in two ways, either in rows or in rounds. Whichever you are doing you must start by making a chain.

This is very simple for it is just a matter of drawing a new loop through the slip loop, and then another loop through that one, and so on. Each loop, as it is replaced on the hook by a new loop, hangs below the hook in a gradually lengthening chain.

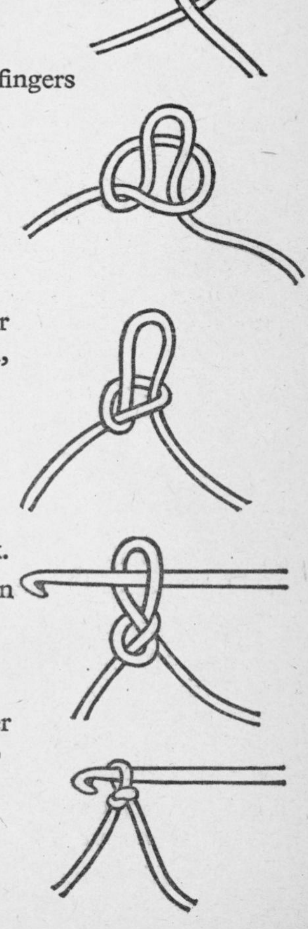

Holding hook and yarn

Hold the hook like a pen in your right hand.

Wrap the yarn round the little finger of your left hand and over the top of your middle finger as the picture shows.

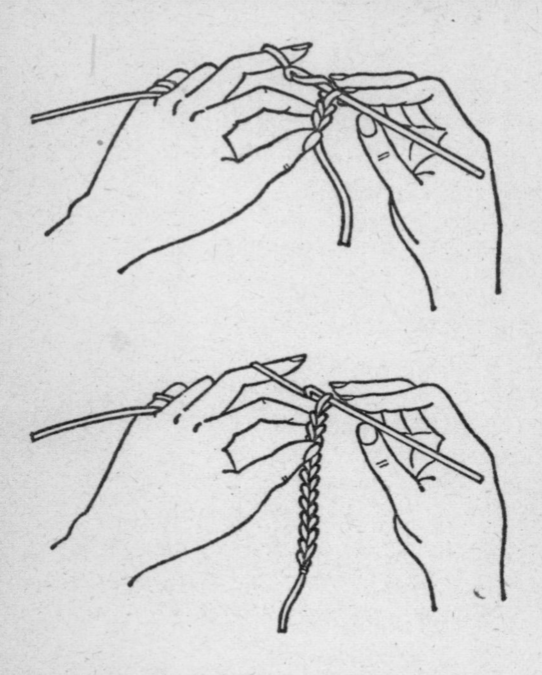

Doing this helps to control the yarn from the ball as you work and stops it from flopping about loose.

It also leaves the thumb and first finger of your left hand free to hold the stiches that have just been worked below the hook, or when you are just beginning you can hold the end of the yarn below the slip loop.

Making a chain

You are ready to start making your first chain.

Put a slip loop on the hook, take the hook in your right hand and put the yarn round your left hand.

Using the tip of the hook, slip it under and behind the yarn that stretches from your second finger to the hook.

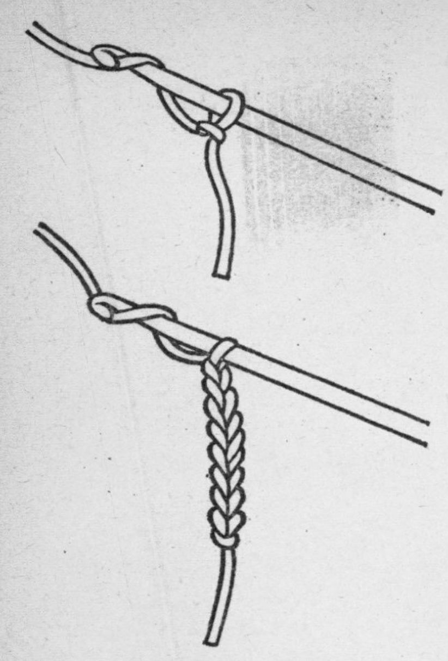

Let the yarn come close to the actual hook in front of the loop that is already on the hook.

Holding the end of the yarn at the base of the first loop firmly between your thumb and first finger of your left hand, draw this new loop through the first one, so that the first one hangs down below it.

Try that again.

Use the tip of the hook to bring the yarn round the hook in front of the loop that is already on it.

Holding the last loop you made with the thumb and finger of your left hand, draw the new loop through.

Go on trying this until you have made quite a long chain.

Do you see how you can keep all the loops lying even and in line with each other if you always hold the work between your left-hand thumb and forefinger as you draw a new loop through the old one ?

If you haven't noticed this it is worth starting again.

Make a new slip knot, just to see if you remember, and then a chain, keeping it from twisting.

If you do let it twist and turn it is more difficult when you come to the next stage, so try and get it nice and even.

You will soon find that it becomes much easier.

You can't practise this too much, for all the time you will be getting used to the feel of the hook, keeping the chains more even and learning to control your left hand which is a very big step towards being able to crochet.

When you feel you can do this easily, and can remember how to make a slip knot also, you can go on to the next step.

Now you can make the chain that you need, either to work in rows as you might for a scarf, or to work in rounds as you would for a table mat that was going to be circular.

Let's try making circles first.

Forming a circle

So far the chains you have made have been straight lines. To make this straight line form a circle you need to join the first stitch to the last stitch and for this we use a stitch called a slip stitch.

A slip stitch is the smallest stitch in crochet and is very simple to make.

Make a slip loop and then work 8 chain.

Curl the chain round so that you can put the hook into the first chain you made.

Now work a slip stitch by putting the yarn round the hook just as you did to form a new chain loop. Check with the diagram if you are not certain.

You will now have the yarn round the hook, just to the right of it the loop of the first stitch, and to the right of that the loop of the last stitch.

Holding the tail of yarn from the slip knot between your left-hand thumb and forefinger, draw the loop through *both* the other loops on the hook.

And now you have a circle.

Try it right from the first slip knot several times before you go on.

Basic stitches

Although there are so many different patterns in crochet there are very few stitches to learn, and already you know two – chain stitch and slip stitch.

Next we are going to learn double crochet stitch and treble crochet stitch.

These two, along with the two you already know, and with another two which are no more difficult, form the basis of all patterns which are simply made from never-ending variations on these six stitches.

Double crochet

Work 8 chain and join into a circle with a slip stitch.

Into this circle you are going to work double crochet stitches.

First work 1 chain.

Now work the first double crochet stitch like this – put the hook through the actual circle and draw the yarn round the hook as you did for a chain stitch.

Bring the hook back through the circle with the yarn and the loop on it.

Put the yarn round the hook again and draw it through the 2 loops already on the hook, and you have made your first double crochet stitch.

Try it again.

Put the hook through the circle and draw the yarn round it.

Now with 2 loops on the hook bring it back through the circle.

Put the yarn round the hook again and draw a new loop through both the loops already on the hook.

Try this 8 times more until there are double crochet stitches all round the circle.

You can complete the circle by joining the last double crochet to the first chain stitch at the beginning of the round by a slip stitch (just as you joined the chain to form a circle, remember ?).

Complete the circle after you have joined it with a slip stitch by cutting the yarn, leaving an end about 8 cm long and drawing it through the slip stitch. Thread the end into a wool needle and darn it nearly into the circle edge before cutting off the unwanted tail.

Make at least 3 more circles with double crochet stitches in them before you go on to the next stitch.

Treble crochet

Make a slip knot and then work 8 chain, joining the chain to form a circle with a slip stitch.

Work 3 chain.

To work the first treble stitch put the yarn round the hook, then put the hook through the circle. Put the yarn round the hook again (3 loops are now on the hook), and draw it back through the circle. Put the yarn round the hook and draw it through 2 of the loops, and then put it round the hook and draw it through the last 2 loops on the hook.

It is really very like a double crochet but has an extra stage added to make it a longer stitch.

Make another treble crochet.

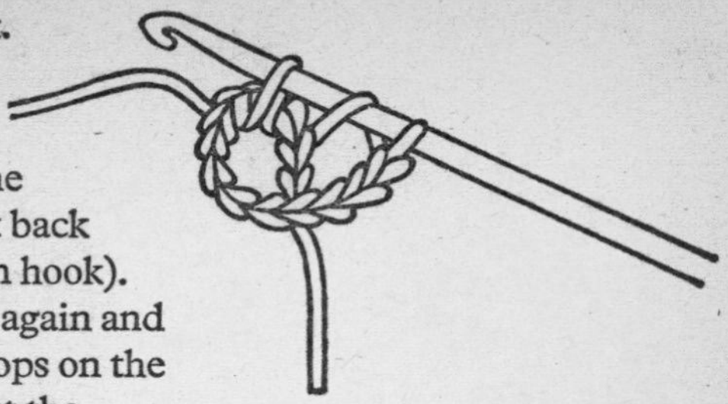

Put the yarn round the hook (2 loops on hook), put it through the circle and put the yarn round again, drawing it back through the circle (3 loops on hook). Put the yarn round the hook again and draw it through the first 2 loops on the hook (leaving 2 loops on). Put the yarn round again and draw it through the last 2 loops.

Work another 8 treble crochet stitches into the circle and finish it off with a slip stitch before cutting the yarn and finishing it off neatly.

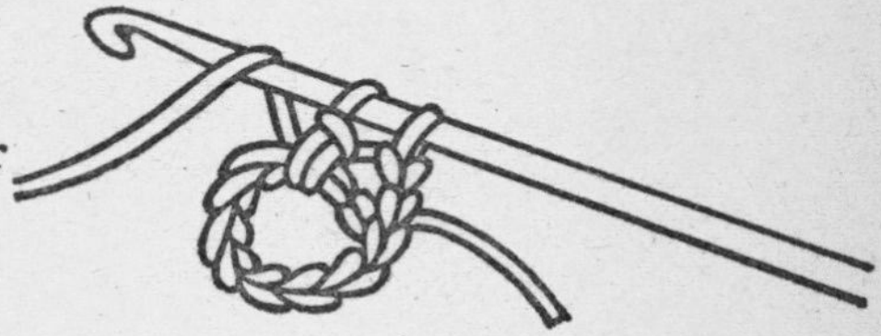

Now you can work 4 different stitches.

You could make a picture for your room to practise what you have learned or you could use chains and circles to decorate a cushion cover.

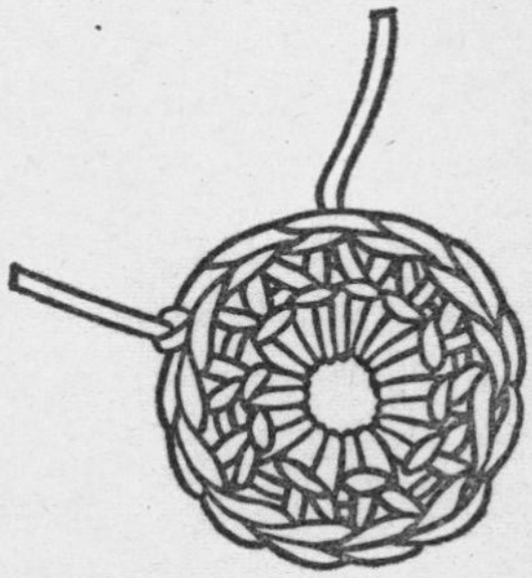

Decorations

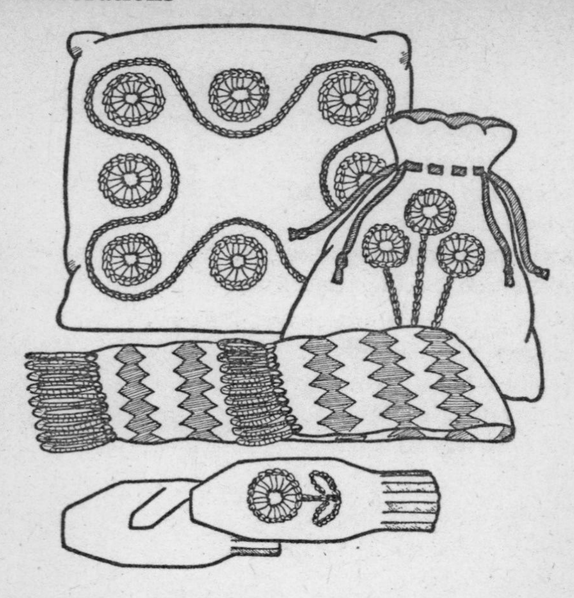

You can use the chains and rings you have made to decorate a plain cushion cover, a material bag, the backs of woollen mitts or gloves, or even the ends of a scarf.

You could arrange the small circles inside the larger ones and outline them with the chains, or you could make the rings look like a bunch of balloons flying high in the sky, each on the end of its own cord.

Perhaps you made or would like to make 2 circles with treble stitches in them. This could be the start of an owl.

A long chain could form his body, a tiny chain his beak and another long brown chain could be the branch he is sitting on.

Don't leave him all alone! A yellow circle filled with double crochet or a yellow chain shaped like a crescent will supply him with the company of the moon.

Sew each circle neatly on to the background with sewing cotton that matches the colour of the wool.

Pin your decorative ideas in place first, just to see if they are exactly what you want.

3 Working things in rows

Before you can really claim that you can crochet, you must be able to work in rows as well as in rounds.

Once again you begin by making a chain and then you work into the actual chain stitches themselves.

Make a chain of 10 stitches.

Now you are going to work along the chain using double crochet.

Working a row

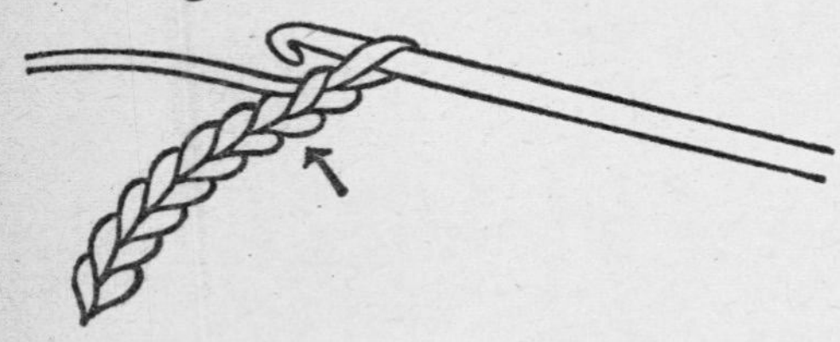

Put the tip of the hook into the second chain from the hook. Check this with the diagram.

Put the yarn round the hook and draw the loop back through the chain stitch (just as you drew it back through the circle when you were working rounds).

Put the yarn round the hook again and draw it through the 2 loops on the hook.

Work into each of the chain stitches in this way, right to the end of the chain.

Did you notice that the diagram showed that you put the hook under both the threads of the chain stitch, not just under one thread?

You will find this is quite easy to do if you took the trouble to learn to make the chain without letting it twist. When it is not twisted it is quite easy to see the even lines of all the stitches along the chain.

When you have worked to the end of the row, check that it looks like the diagram before you start the next row. If you are not certain, start again and try it until you are sure you can manage it.

To start the next row you must turn the work round so that the loop of the last stitch is still on the hook at the right-hand corner of the work.

Work 1 chain and then work 1 double crochet stitch into the top of the second stitch and every stitch to the end of the row, putting the hook through both top loops of every stitch.

Try several rows more, starting each row with 1 chain stitch.

It is just as easy to work rows of treble crochet, so let's try that next.

Working treble crochet in rows

Work 12 chain stitches.

Put the yarn round the hook and then insert it into the fourth chain from the hook.

Put the yarn round the hook and draw it through the chain stitch. You will have 3 loops on the hook now.

Put the yarn round the hook again, and draw it through the first 2 loops, and then put the yarn round the hook once more and draw it through the last 2 loops on the hook.

Work into each chain stitch to the end of the row in this way.

When the row is complete turn the work so that the loop on the hook is at the right-hand end.

To start the second row work 3 chain, then work 1 treble into the second stitch and into every stitch to the end of the row.

Try several more rows beginning each row with 3 chain.

Count the number of stitches in the last row and see if it is the same number of stitches that you had after the first row. You can count the 3 chain at the beginning of the row as 1 stitch.

If you have more stitches or less stitches than you had on the first row start again and try and keep the same number of stitches so that the edges of your crochet remain straight.

Now you are certainly getting on but there is one thing that we must notice before we go any further.

When you started a row of double crochet you worked 1 chain first, and when you worked treble crochet you began each row with 3 chain stitches.

Did you wonder why?

These stitches are called the 'turning' chain and are needed to get your hook up to the top level of the row ready for the next stitch.

Turning chain

Starting a row with a treble would mean that it was pulled over sideways instead of being its correct height. By working chain stitches to take the place of the first stitch you can get round this problem.

Each type of stitch has its own number of turning chain. Here is a table which gives the number of turning chain for each type of stitch:

double crochet	1 turning chain
half treble crochet	2 turning chain
treble crochet	3 turning chain
double treble crochet	4 turning chain
triple treble crochet	5 turning chain
quadruple treble crochet	6 turning chain

You have not worked all these stitches yet, but when do you, if you need to check how many turning chain you will need, remember to look at that page.

Turning chain are, in this book, always given at the beginning of a row in the instructions for the simple reason that they are counted as the first stitch.

In some patterns and books giving instructions for crochet you will find that the chain for the turning chain is given at the end of a row before you turn the work round.

It serves just the same purpose so don't let this difference worry you.

Turning chain are just as necessary when you are working rounds as in rows.

It is usual to find that after you have worked a slip stitch to join the last stitch with the first of a round the next round begins with one or more chain, depending on the stitch that is being used, and it will also count as the first stitch in the round.

When the round is finished the joining slip stitch will be worked into the top of this chain. If the chain was of 3 stitches then the slip stitch will be worked into the third of these stitches.

Working half treble

Before we go on to more exciting things like working with more than one colour and shaping the things we make let's learn to work half treble.

You can't say you can't do it because it is so like what you have done already in learning double crochet and treble crochet.

Work 12 chain.

Put the yarn round the hook and put it into the third chain from the hook.

Put the yarn round the hook and draw it back through the chain. So far it is exactly like a treble crochet.

Put the yarn round the hook and draw it through all the loops at once, instead of drawing it through 2 loops and then another 2 as you did for treble crochet.

Try it again.

Put the yarn round the hook and insert it through both loops of the next stitch. Put the yarn round the hook and draw it through. Yarn round hook and draw it through all the loops on the hook.

Work to the end of the row in this way, working a half treble into each chain stitch.

When you are ready to start the second row check back to see how many turning chain you need.

Hairband

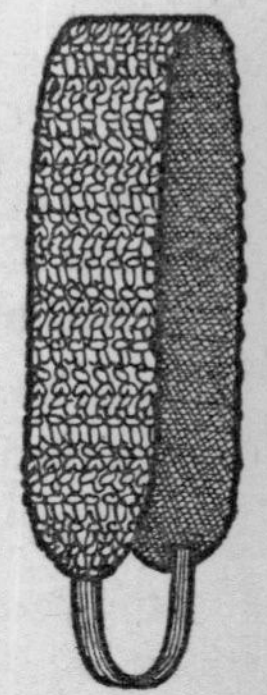

A very good way of practising working in rows and using the treble stitch you have just learnt is to make yourself a hairband.

You will need:
1 ball (25-g) Patons Trident Double Knitting
1 crochet hook size 4.50
Short length narrow elastic, about 20 cm

To work the hairband
Begin by making 9 chain.

1st row Work 1 treble into 4th chain from hook, work 1 treble into each of the next 5 chain stitches. Turn.

2nd row 3 chain, work 1 treble into the 2nd stitch and into each of the other stitches to the end of the row (7 stitches, counting the turning chain as 1 stitch).

3rd row 3 chain, 1 treble into each stitch to the end. The last stitch is worked into the 3rd chain of the turning chain. Counting the turning chain as 1 stitch you will again have 7 stitches.

Continue repeating the 3rd row until the band is long enough to reach round your head, leaving just over a 20-cm gap for the elastic at the centre back.

Count the number of stitches every 10 rows or so to see that you are not making or losing any stitches.

When the band is the right length cut the yarn, leaving a tail to darn in, and draw the end through the last stitch.

Darn in the end and cut away any unwanted ends.

Sew the elastic to either end of the band so that you have formed a circle.

4 Striping things

Already you can make things and you can work five different stitches. Now if you learn to add different colours and work in wide or narrow stripes you are beginning to give yourself the possibility of lots of interesting things to make.

Really wide stripes of 10 cm or more, such as you might find on a scarf, are best worked by joining in the required colour for that section and finishing it off neatly when another colour is wanted.

Narrow stripes can be worked by carrying the yarn up the side of the work until it is required again, so that you are not always joining and rejoining the different colours.

Whichever type of stripe, the first thing you must learn is how to join in a different colour or a new ball of yarn.

Joining yarn

The very best place to join yarn is at the side edge, although you can only do this when you are working in rows. Circles we will deal with shortly.

Some books will show you how to place both ends together along the actual stitch tops and work the next few stitches over them, securing them in place.

Although this is possible it also makes a small bump in the work and can be avoided, even if you want to change colours in the middle of a row.

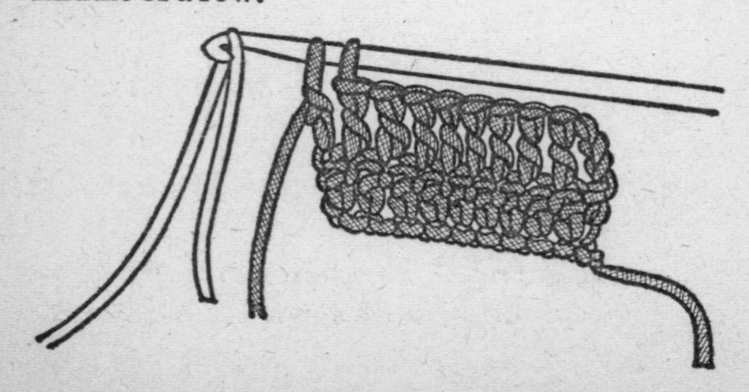

Work to the last stitch that is to be in the first colour, colour A, then complete all but the final stage of the last stitch. If you are working in double crochet this would mean that you had put the yarn round the hook and drawn it back through the stitch.

Leave colour A hanging and put the second colour, colour B, over the hook leaving a short end hanging. Now complete the stitch in the usual way but using colour B. Both ends can be darned into the wrong side of the work afterwards.

Treble crochet in two colours

Try a small sample in treble crochet using 2 colours.
Work 2 rows of 10 trebles in the first colour.

On the next row work until there is only 1 stitch left to make.

Put the yarn round the hook, put the hook into the last stitch, put the yarn round the hook and draw it through, put the yarn round the hook and draw it through 2 loops on the hook. Now you have just the last stage of the treble to work.

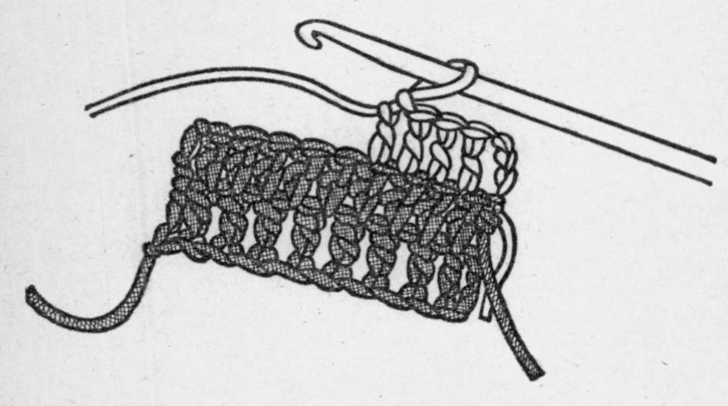

Leave the colour you have been using hanging, and take the end of the second colour. Put it over the hook, leaving a tail of about 10 cm, and complete the last stage of the stitch.

Wonder why you can't join at the beginning of a stitch instead of halfway through?

Try it and you will quickly see. The join will show a little way up the stitch. Whereas working another colour in during the last stage of the stitch allows the colour you are finishing with to form the whole of the last stitch.

If you are working a coloured motif or pattern that requires changing to the new colour during the row, work it in this way.

You could also join in a new ball of the same colour in this way but avoid doing so if possible. Watch how much yarn is left and begin a new ball at the end of a row so that you are not darning in extra ends in the middle of your work – even if they are neat and on the wrong side.

Joining yarn in a circle

Because it is never possible to join yarn except in the middle of the work when you are working in rounds you can use this same method or you can finish off after you have worked the slip stitch joining the beginning and end of the round.

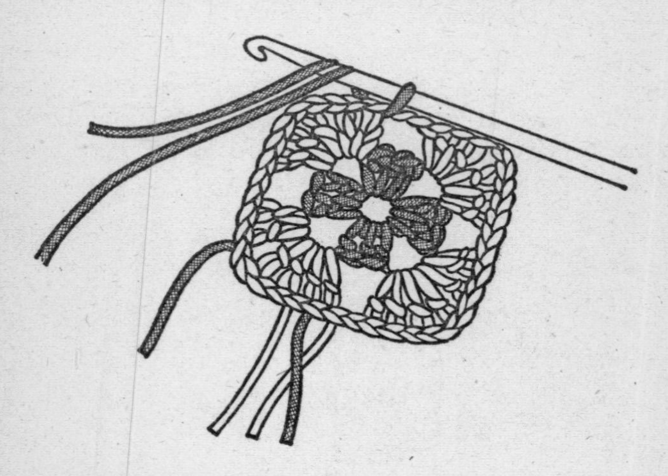

Put the hook into the next stitch (it is likely to be into the same place as the joining slip stitch, depending on your pattern), put a loop of the new ball or next colour over the hook and draw it through, work the next chain using both ends of the yarn so that it is locked in place and then continue with the single yarn.

Narrow stripes

Narrow stripes may mean that you can leave 1 colour hanging at the side edge for 2 or at the most 3 rows before you use it again. If you are using 2 colours and are working 2 rows in each colour you will be able to carry the colours up the edge of the work. Also if you are using 3 colours and are working up to 2 rows of each colour you can do the same.

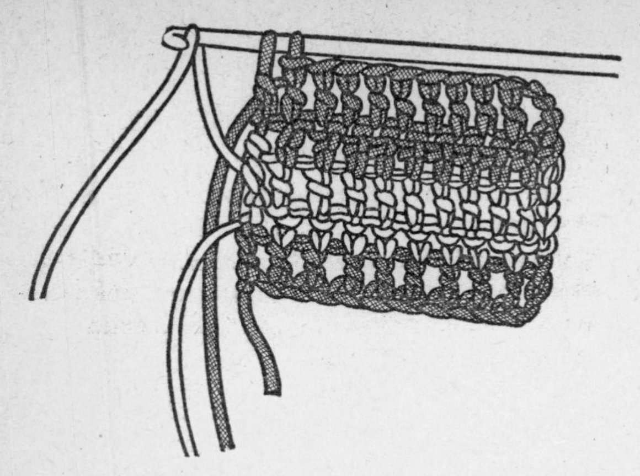

Start the new colour in the same way as shown above by working the last stage of the last stitch of a row with it, leaving the colour you have just finished hanging at the side.

When you take any colour up the side across row ends be very careful not to drag the work and pull the side tight. The yarn carried up the side must just sit neatly against the row ends, not being tight nor in slack loops that will work loose.

Drawstring purse

This little purse, which is about 12 cm deep when it is finished, will give you a chance to practise joining in different coloured yarns to make stripes.

It is worked in half treble stitch.

You will need:
2 colours of Patons Trident Double Knitting (A and B)
1 crochet hook size 4.50

To work the drawstring purse

Using colour A work 26 chain.

1st row Into the 3rd chain from hook work 1 half treble, 1 half treble in each chain to end (25 stitches). Turn.

2nd row 2 chain, work 1 half treble in each stitch until there is only one left to work into the turning chain. Work until there is only one stage of this stitch left to make. Join in colour B (leaving colour A hanging at the side) and complete the stitch.

3rd row Using B make 2 chain, 1 half treble in each stitch to the end.

4th row 2 chain, 1 half treble in each stitch until only 1 stitch is left to work. Work all of it except the last stage, leave B at the side and pick up A again, completing the stitch.

Work 2 rows more in A, 2 rows in B, 2 rows in A, 2 rows in B, joining in A again on the last stitch.

Work 1 more row of A in half trebles.

Next row 3 chain (1 chain, miss 1 stitch, 1 treble in next stitch), repeat the stitches in brackets right along the row. Turn.

Last row 1 chain, 1 double crochet into each stitch to the end (that is 1 double crochet in each space made by the 1 chain and 1 double crochet in each treble stitch). Cut the thread and finish off the ends.

To make up

Fold the bag in half and join the side seam and the bottom edge. Work 2 chains of 40 stitches each in colour B. Thread both of them through the slots and sew the ends together making two separate circles to pull the purse shut.

5 Making things easier

Now that you can manage so much and have made some things it is time you learned the language of crochet.

You have made things and you have learned the stitch names but the pages in the book are rapidly getting filled up with all the words that are being used to explain what to do next, especially when instructions for things to make are being given.

There are shorter ways of explaining, which are also simpler to use because they are quicker to read.

The first thing to do is shorten the names of the stitches, and this is done by the use of abbreviations.

Abbreviations

Abbreviations are what we call words that are shortened.

This is what happens:

Chain stitch becomes	ch
Slip stitch becomes	ss
Double crochet becomes	dc
Half treble crochet becomes	htr
Treble crochet becomes	tr

3 other stitches which you have not learned yet – double treble, triple treble and quadruple treble – but which you will learn soon, can also be abbreviated:

Double treble stitch becomes	dtr
Triple treble stitch becomes	tr tr
Quadruple treble becomes	quad tr

You can really see at a glance from their abbreviation just which each stitch is, and you will very quickly learn these abbreviations.

But there are other words that are used many times that can be shortened also. Here is a list of these:

Stitch(es) becomes	st(s)
Metre(s) becomes	m
Centimetre(s) becomes	cm
Millimetre(s) becomes	mm
Gramme(s) becomes	g
Yarn round hook becomes	yrh
Continue becomes	cont
Repeat becomes	rep
Space becomes	sp
Increase becomes	inc
Decrease becomes	dec
Beginning (or begin) becomes	beg
Pattern becomes	patt
Remain becomes	rem
Alternate becomes	alt

All instructions in leaflets and books will give you a list of the abbreviations that they use, and if they use more unusual ones they will always be fully explained. Sometimes the instructions deal with groups of stitches, or clusters, and it can help to abbreviate any word that will come up often.

The asterisk or star

Until now you have been told exactly what to do, step by step. But in some rows or rounds the same thing is repeated several times over. Instead of writing such steps fully every time they are written only once and an asterisk, which is this star *, is placed before it.

After the asterisk come the words describing what you have to do, followed by clear instructions of how many times you go back to the * and repeat in your crochet what the words tell you to do.

Sometimes you may find that repeats are placed inside brackets ( ), but again you would be told outside the brackets how many times you are expected to work the repeat, or if you simply repeat what is in the brackets until the end of the row or round is reached.

In this book we have used brackets in a different way, always using an * to mark repeats.

Sometimes you want to work several times into the same stitch and you will find that this is mostly how we have used brackets.

It might be that into 1 stitch you want to work a treble followed by 2 chain and then another treble into the same stitch and 3 chain and again another treble.

All this would be indicated by the words 'into the next stitch work (1tr, 2ch, 1tr, 3ch, 1tr)'. You must admit it is easier to write in this form and much easier to read because there is so much less of it to look at.

Other things to know about instructions

Before instructions begin you will usually find several things set out for you.

There will be a short list of all the 'Materials' that you need to make the article. The size of crochet hook, the amount of yarn, the type of yarn, and anything required to complete the design like elastic, ribbon, buttons or zip.

There will also be a section headed 'Measurements' and another called 'Tension'.

Materials

Apart from helping you to have everything ready for the design you are going to make, this section on materials helps in two other ways.

It tells you which yarn the designer used and how much was used. If you use a different yarn you needn't expect the result to be the same. Buy exactly what the instructions suggest and then you will be much more likely to be pleased with the result.

One beginner quite spoiled a waistcoat by thinking that all yarns called Arran must be the same and she didn't try to get Arran wool made by the spinner that was mentioned in the 'Materials'. She bought some in the market and it turned out to be made from nylon which was also only about half as thick as the yarn she should have bought.

You are also told how much yarn to buy and it is a good idea to buy all you need at once so that you get balls that have all been dyed at the same time. Batches of yarn dyed at different times may vary very slightly in colour and spoil your work by giving it a slightly striped effect – when you don't want it!

The size of the crochet hook used is also important. This is the size that the designer used. But not everybody crochets in the same way. Some people do pull the stitches very tight and others always have loose stitches. Whichever you do it is right for you and it is better to change the hook size than try to alter the way you hold the yarn. If your stitches are very slack then you will be helped by using a finer hook than is suggested, and if the stitches are packed tightly together a larger hook will help to make the work more open.

This is why in designs where the size matters there is a section called 'Tension'.

Tension

Tension is the number of stitches that the designer had over whatever measurement is given. It may be the number of stitches in 5 cm, in 10 cm, or in 20 cm or even in 2 or 4 inches. The important thing is that you manage to get the same number of stitches to the measurement as the designer did, changing the hook size if you need to.

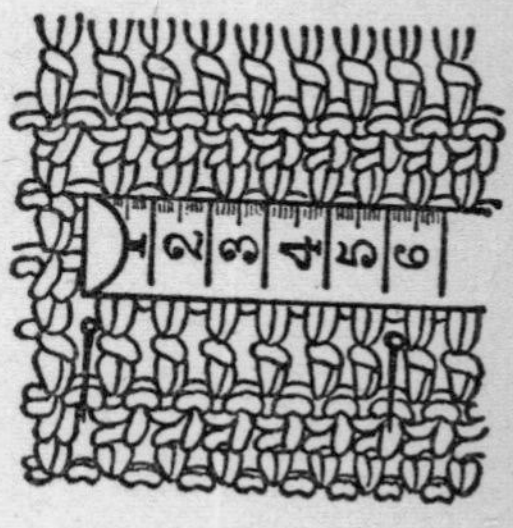

It is usually because the tension hasn't been checked, but simply ignored and skipped over, that things go wrong or don't look the same as the designer intended.

So before you start to make anything, check to see if the tension is mentioned. If it is, then use the hook and yarn stated and see if you get the same tension. If you don't, alter the hook size and try again.

Once you get the tension correct you are well on the way to making something which you can be proud of and which won't give you any trouble, either to make, or as far as its finished size is concerned.

Measurements

The section headed 'Measurements' is also important because it gives you an idea of the finished size. It is no use starting to make mittens for yourself if the measurements tell you quite clearly that when they are finished they will only fit a toddler.

Always check that the size is the size you want.

Also when you come to sewing up the garment or article it is useful to know the finished size because it can help when it comes to pinning the pieces out to press.

Why not try and make a useful and traditional granny square from the following instructions which use all the shortened forms of words we have been learning about.

Although this square starts as a circle it gradually becomes square and is very simple to work. Join in the different colours as you learned to do in Chapter 4 when you joined in a new colour at the beginning of the round after completing the previous round with a slip stitch and finishing off. Granny squares can then be sewn together to make lots of lovely things for you.

Granny squares

Materials

Balls of 2, 3 or 4 colours of Patons Double Knitting or Patons Trident Double Knitting
1 crochet hook size 4.50

Measurements

One square of 4 rounds will measure about 10 cm

To work the square

With 1st colour: work 6ch. Join with ss to form circle.

1st round 3ch, 2tr into circle, *1ch, 3tr into circle, rep from * twice more, 1ch, join with ss to 3rd of first 3ch. Cut yarn leaving end to darn in.

2nd round Join 2nd colour into any 1ch sp, 3ch, into same space work (2tr, 1ch, 3tr), 1ch, * into next 1ch sp work (3tr, 1ch, 3tr), 1ch, rep from * twice more. Join with ss to 3rd of first 3ch. Cut yarn.

3rd round Into 1ch sp to left of ss join 1st colour, 3ch, into same sp work (2tr, 1ch, 3tr), 1ch,* into next sp work 3tr, 1ch, into next sp, which is a corner, work (3tr, 1ch, 3tr), 1ch, rep from * twice more, into next sp work 3tr, 1ch, join with ss into 3rd of first 3ch. Cut yarn.

4th round Into corner 1ch sp join 2nd colour, 3ch, into same sp work (2tr, 1ch, 3tr), 1ch, * into next space, a side sp, work 3tr, 1ch, into next sp work 3tr, 1ch, into next corner sp work (3tr, 1ch 3tr), 1ch, rep from * twice more, into next sp work 3tr,

1ch, into last side sp work 3tr, 1ch, join with ss. Finish off all ends.

This completes the traditional square, many of which are joined together to make whatever you want, from a pot holder or mat to a bedspread.

But you can also go on adding other rounds to make the square larger. Each round will have one more group of stitches on each side than the round before. This can make a very nice cushion cover by making 2 big squares or even a nightdress case for yourself or as a present for a friend.

You can make 2 squares each with 11 rounds from 2 (25-g) balls of Patons Trident Double Knitting using only 2 colours or, if you want to use 4 colours you will need 1 ball in each of the 4 colours.

You can see how to crochet the squares together instead of sewing them together in Chapter 8.

6 Shaping things bigger

So far you have only made rounds or things that have had straight sides, strips or squares. Giving shape to the things you make is very important. because only when you can do this can you make exactly the sizes you want.

When you add stitches to make your work grow bigger it is called 'increasing' and the added stitches are 'increases'.

When you want to make work smaller then you 'decrease' and the stitches that do this are called 'decreases'.

Two ways of increasing in rows

There are two ways in which work may be made bigger when you are working in rows.

The first way is used most often when you want to add quite a lot of stitches at the side of the work, as you might want to do if you

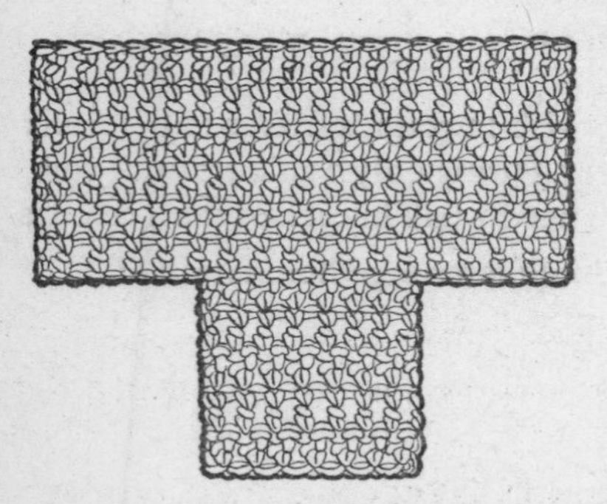

were making a shape like the diagram. This might be for a bonnet or hat, for a baby's slipper, or a doll's dress, or even if you were making a summer top and wanted to add stitches for a small sleeve.

Work up to the point where the stitches are needed and at the end of the row add as many chains as you need stitches. Turn, and work into the chain on the next row to make the new stitches.

When you want to add stitches at both ends you need to work a chain at one side, turn, work into the chain and then add another similar chain at the end of that row. Turn and work into this

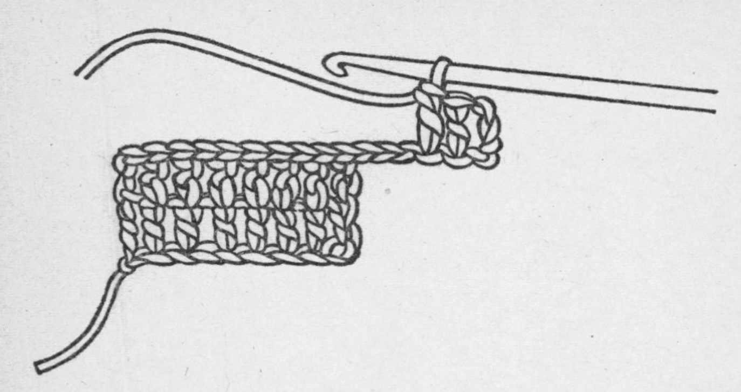

chain and right across to the end of the row which now includes the new stitches at the end as well.

What happens if you want to add 1 stitch at each end of every fourth row, or even every other row?

You get an edge that is like a staircase, don't you.

If these edges are going to be sewn together you are giving yourself a problem because the seam is not a nice straight line.

Because of this there is another method of increasing when it is only single stitches at the side of the work unless, of course, the 'step' is part of the design and is the way you want the finished work to be.

Single increases

Where side edges are to be joined or where you want to have a neat gradual slope you can increase by working 2 stitches into the top of the same stitch.

Work until there are 2 stitches left to work on a row of double, half treble or treble crochet.
Work once into the next stitch and then again before working the final stitch.

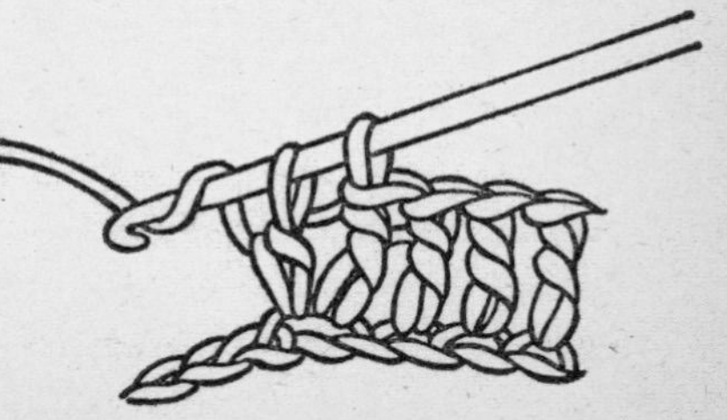

In this way you will have increased 1 stitch. Work 1 row without adding any stitches. Now work again to the last 2 stitches. Work 2 stitches into the next stitch and then work the final stitch. Work another row without adding any stitches.

Now you should begin to see that the stitches are making the side edge slope outwards.

This type of increase can be worked at either end of the row or anywhere along the row that it is required.

Increasing in rounds

Adding stitches when you are working in rounds is done in exactly the same way, by working 2 or even more times into the top of the same stitch, or if it is a patterned round like the granny square, the extra stitches may all be worked into the same space.

Do you remember the first circles you made?

If you had gone on in rounds with the same number of stitches in each round you would have crocheted a tube. To make a flat circle the edge has to grow in length with each round by increasing. Too many increases and it will get frilly, because the outside edge gets larger than the rest of the circle; it would become tube-like if the outside edge is too small.

Making a flat circle

Work 6 ch. Join first and last stitches with a ss to form a circle.

1st round 3ch, work 9tr into circle. Join with a ss to 3rd of first of 3ch.

2nd round 3ch, 1tr into same st as ch, * 2tr into next st, rep from * to end of round, join with ss. (This might have been written: 2 tr into each st.)

3rd round 3 ch, 1tr into same st as ch, 1tr into next st, * 2tr into next st, 1tr into next st, rep from * to end of round, join with ss. (This could have been: increase in every alternate st, or work twice into every other st.) You should now have 30 trebles in the round.

4th round 3ch, 1tr into same st as ch, 1tr into each of next 2sts,* 2tr into next st, 1tr into each of next 2 sts, rep from * to end, join with ss. (This might have been: increase in every 3rd st.) You will quickly find that there are many different types of circles.

If the increases are always worked immediately above each other the circle will keep growing and stay flat but the edges between the increases will begin to be straight.
The number of edges will depend on the number of increases. 8 evenly spaced increases will give you a shape with 8 even sides.

If the 8 increases are arranged so that 2 are placed together, then there is a space and then another pair, evenly 4 times round the circle, you will begin to get a square shape.

A round circle will need to have the increases out of line with each other so that the edge remains round.
There is also another way of making a round grow bigger. It may not be the actual upright treble or double crochet stitches that you increase. If you have trebles with a chain stitch between, and you add to the chain stitches working 2 chain between the trebles and then in later rounds 3 chain and 4 chain, you will get a cobweb effect which is used a great deal in designing lacy mats and circular designs.

Now you can make something round. Why not try a mat?

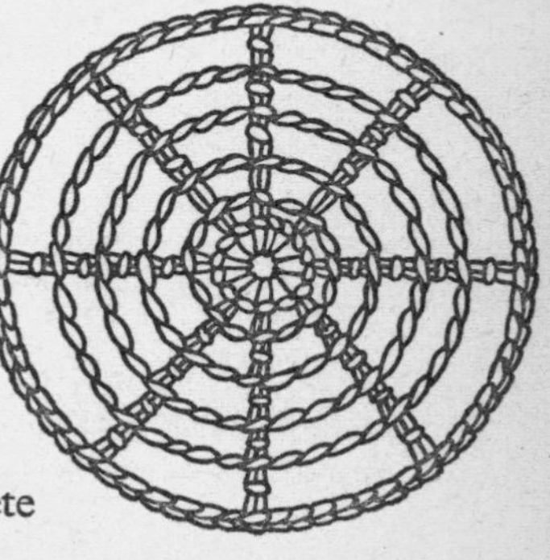

Round mat

Materials

1 (25-g) ball of Patons Trident Double Knitting
1 crochet hook size 4.50

Measurements

About 24 cm across centre when complete

To work the mat

Work 4ch. Join with ss to form circle.

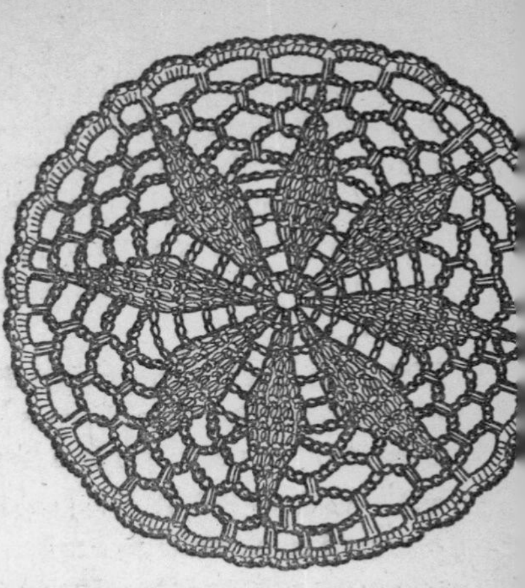

1st round 6ch,* 1tr into circle, 3 ch, rep from * 6 times more. Join with ss to 3rd of first 6ch.

2nd round 3ch, 2tr in same st as ch, 1ch, * 3tr in next tr, 1ch, rep from * 6 times more. Join with ss to 3rd of first 3ch.

3rd round 3ch, 3tr in next tr, 1tr in next tr, 2ch, * 1tr in next tr, 3tr in centre tr, 1tr in next tr, 2ch, rep from * 6 times more. Join with ss to 3rd of first 3ch.

4th round 3ch, 1tr in next tr, 3tr in centre tr, 1tr in each of next 2tr, 3ch,* 1tr in each of next 2tr, 3tr in centre tr, 1tr in each of next 2tr, 3ch, rep from * 6 times more. Join with ss to 3rd of 3ch.

5th round 3ch, 1tr in each of next 6tr, 5ch,* 1tr in each of next 7tr, 5ch, rep from * 6 times more. Join with ss to 3rd of 3ch.

6th round Ss in next tr, 3ch, 1tr in each of next 4tr, 5ch, 1dc in 5ch sp, 5ch,* miss 1tr, 1tr in each of next 5tr, 5ch, 1dc in 5ch sp, 5ch, rep from * 6 times more. Join with ss to 3rd of 3ch.

7th round Ss in next tr, 3ch, 1tr in each of next 2tr (5ch, 1dc into next 5ch sp) twice, 5ch,* miss 1tr, 1tr in each of next 3tr (5ch, 1dc into next 5ch sp) twice, 5ch, rep from * 6 times more. Join with ss in 3rd of 3ch.

8th round Ss in next tr, 8ch (1dc into next 5ch sp, 5ch) 3 times,* miss 1tr, 1tr in centre tr, (5ch, 1dc in next 5ch sp) 3 times, 5ch, rep from * 6 times more. Join with ss in 3rd of 8ch.

9th round Ss in next 3ch to centre of loop, * 5ch, 1dc in next 5ch sp, rep from * round circle. Join with ss in first ch.

10th round Into each 5ch sp work (1dc, 1htr, 1tr, 1htr, 1dc). Join with ss to first dc. Cut yarn and finish off ends.

See Chapter 9 for help with pressing the finished mat.

Work until 3 treble stitches are left. Put the yarn round the hook, put it through the next stitch, put the yarn round the hook and draw it through the stitch, put the yarn round the hook and draw it through 2 loops. Now do that also into the next stitch.

You will now have 3 loops on the hook. Put the yarn round and pull it through all the loops together. Again you will have 2 stitches at the base but will have joined the tops together into 1 stitch.

Decreasing in rounds

Decreasing in rounds is usually worked in just the same way as in rows, by working 2 stitches together.

Just as with increasing there is also the possibility of working gradually fewer chain stitches between the actual treble or other upright stitches and so gradually making the circle smaller.

Practice in both increasing and decreasing can be had in making a ball. You can easily experiment with it. Try striping it or working it in half one colour and half another colour. The ball is perfect for a toddler to play with.

It isn't even very difficult to make balls of different sizes; then you can put them together to make clowns and snowmen and all sorts of fun people.

Ball

Materials

1 (25-g) ball of Patons Trident Double Knitting
1 crochet hook size 4.50
Kapok for stuffing, or foam chips

Measurements

About 30 cm round when complete

To work the ball

Work 6ch. Join with ss to form circle.

1st round 3ch, work 15tr into circle. Join with ss into 3rd of 3ch. (16 sts)

2nd round 3ch, 1tr into next tr, * 2tr in next tr, 1tr in next tr, rep from * to end of round. Join with ss. (23 sts)

3rd round 3ch, * 2tr in next tr, 1tr in next tr, rep from * to end of round. Join with ss. (34 sts)

4th round 3ch, 1tr in next tr, * 2tr in next tr, 1tr in each of next 3tr, rep from * to end of round. Join with ss. (42 sts)

5th round 3ch, 1tr in each tr to end of round. Join with ss.

6th, 7th, 8th and 9th rounds Work as given for 5th round.

10th round 3ch, 1tr in next tr, * dec 1tr by working first half of next 2 sts then working the sts together, 1tr in each of next 3tr, rep from * to end of round. Join with ss.

11th round 3ch, * dec in next 2 sts, 1tr in next tr, rep from * to end of round. Join with ss.

12th round 3ch, 1tr in next tr * dec in next 2 sts, 1tr in next tr, rep from * to end of round. Join with ss.

Remove hook from loop and fill the ball with Kapok before working the final round.

Last round 3ch, 1tr in each tr. Join with ss. Cut yarn leaving a 15-cm end. Thread into wool needle and darn the end round the last row. Draw up and darn in the ends.

8 Making things with motifs

Sometimes a pram rug or a scarf can seem quite a big thing to tackle when you are thinking about it before you actually begin. There is one way in which big things get made quite quickly without you even noticing their size and that is by making them in motifs.

Each motif is made separately and sewn together once you have enough to make what you want. Almost everything can be made this way, from a small belt to a really large rug.

In fact you have already seen this if you think back to the granny squares in Chapter 5. Several of these small squares could be sewn together to make a hat, a few more will make a doll's pram cover or a cushion cover and some more could make a scarf.

This is just a start and you will find that motifs come in all shapes and sizes and can be made in all shades.

Many are worked in rows but a great many are worked in rounds, some starting round and staying round when they are finished, others starting round and becoming square like the granny square.

Your favourite motif can be given a different appearance by changing the colour scheme.

Think about the granny square for a moment. One design might have each round in each square a different colour. Perhaps the first round white, the second round lemon, the third round orange, the fourth round all dark green.

But you could vary this by making half the squares like this and the other half starting with dark green, then orange, then lemon and finishing with white on the outside. If you sewed them together so that one in one colour was always next to one in another it would make a very different effect from the first colour scheme.

Try out a few ideas for yourself.

It is quite a good idea not to leave all the sewing together until the end. Darn some of the ends in and tidy up the motifs when you have a few spare moments and perhaps not enough time to work a whole motif. This way when you have enough motifs for what you want to make you won't have such a big job to face.

Crochet the motifs together

Possibly by now you like crocheting better than sewing. In that case why not try crocheting the motifs together ? It is very easy and is much the quickest way, provided the motif has an even edge like a granny square.

You can join the squares on the right side so that each becomes framed by a neat ridge which can be the same colour as the background, or you could really make it look like a frame by using a contrasting colour. If you are actually joining squares which all have the same-coloured centres but the edges are in a different colour, perhaps you could use the centre colour for the ridge.

When you want the joining to show less you can work it on the wrong side so that it shows very little apart from serving to join the squares together.

Right side joining

Place the two squares together wrong sides touching and insert the hook through the back loop only of the corner stitch on both squares.

Put the yarn round the hook and draw it through, put the yarn round the hook again and complete the double crochet stitch by drawing the yarn through both loops. Repeat this through each stitch along the edges to the next corner, making certain that you match the stitches exactly, keeping the squares even. Cut the yarn and draw it through the last stitch.

Perhaps you are making a pram rug 5 squares wide by 7 squares long.

Join 7 squares in this way so that you have a long strip with the edges of each square joined to the next. When you have 2 strips of 7 squares join the 2 strips.

When you join 2 strips you work in just the same way but you don't have to do each square separately. You can work right down the strip to the other end without having to cut the yarn and rejoin it.

Wrong side joining

Place the right sides of 2 squares together and join the yarn to the first stitch by placing the hook through both loops of each corner stitch. Put the yarn round the hook and draw it through, work 1 chain.

Work along the sides of the square using slip stitches through both loops of each square. As you have not used slip stitches in this way let's go step by step.

Put the hook through both loops of the second stitches on both squares.

Put the yarn round the hook and draw it through the stitches and through the loop on the hook all at once.

Work the next stitch in the same way. The one thing you must be careful of is that you don't pull the stitches too tight. It is very easy to do this so you need to pull the yarn through a little more than you might normally do.

Your finished work won't look very nice if the seams of each square are tight and are smaller than the squares themselves.

Whichever method you use, finish off all the ends afterwards.

Party stole – made by working motifs together

Some motifs are designed so that you actually crochet them together as you are working them. This has one very great advantage for as you complete the last motif your work is finished except for ends to darn in.
Here is a motif which has been specially designed for you so that you can try this for yourself.
The first motif is complete in itself. When the second motif is made it is almost the same as the first except for one side where, at both corners and in the centre of the side, it is joined to the first motif.
This motif was then used to make a very pretty party stole.

Materials
6 (20-g) balls Patons Double Plus
1 crochet hook size 5.00

To work and join the motifs

First motif

Work 8ch. Join with ss to form a circle.

1st round 6ch, * 1tr into circle, 3ch, rep from * 6 times more. Join with ss to 3rd of 6ch.

2nd round 3ch, 3tr in 3ch sp, * 1tr in next tr, 3 tr in next 3ch sp, rep from * 6 times more. Join with ss to 3rd of 3ch.

3rd round 10ch, * miss 1tr, 1dc in each of next 3tr, 3ch, miss 1tr, 1dc in each of next 3tr, 9ch, rep from * twice more, miss 1tr, 1dc in each of next 3tr, 3ch, miss 1tr, 1dc in each of next 2 tr, join with ss to first of 10ch. Cut yarn and finish off.

Second motif

Work in same way as for first motif to end of 2nd round.

3rd round 5ch, work 1ss in centre st of 9ch loop on first motif, 4ch, on 2nd motif miss 1tr, 1dc in each of next 3tr, 1ch, 1ss in centre st of next 3ch sp on first motif, 1ch, on second motif miss 1tr, 1dc in each of next 3tr, 4ch, 1ss in centre st of 9ch loop on first motif (now you have joined the two motifs through two corners and one side, complete the second motif only), 4ch, * miss 1tr 1dc in each of next 3tr, 3ch, miss 1tr, 1dc in each of next 3tr, 9ch, rep from * once more, miss 1tr, 1dc in each of next 3tr, 3ch, miss 1tr, 1dc in each of next 2tr, join with ss to first of 5ch. Cut yarn and finish off ends.

The first motif and the second are joined on one side only. Once you have joined as many motifs as you want you will need to start a second row.

The first motif of the second row will be joined to the first motif of the first strip on one side only but the motif next to it will be joined on two sides.

It should be quite easy for you to see how to do this for it is really far more simple than it sounds in words, as you will agree when you try it.

The party stole was made from 12 rows, each having 5 motifs.

9 Finishing things off

Finishing the things you make is quite an important stage and should never be neglected.

When you have reached this point check the ball band of the yarn you have used before you do anything else. Here you will find information that will help you to know whether you should press your work with a damp cloth and a warm iron, a cool iron over a dry cloth, or leave the work unpressed altogether.

Remember it will only help you if you do look at the ball band *before* you start to press the work. If you have already laid a hot iron on yarn that should not have been pressed at all then we're afraid it will take more than a ball band to rescue your work!

Pure wool can always be pressed with a warm iron held lightly over a damp cloth. The ball band will show an iron with 2 dots inside it when a warm iron should be used.

Most completely man-made fibres require pressing with a cool iron over a dry cloth. The ball band will carry the symbol of an iron with 1 dot inside it when a cool iron should be used.

Some yarns must not be pressed at all. When this is so the ball band will carry the symbol of an iron with a large X through it.

The other symbols which will help you are those which show how to wash the yarn and also whether it can be bleached or dry cleaned, or not.

Here is a table which shows you the symbols and what they mean, together with an example of how they might appear on a ball band.

Pressing

To press any crochet lay the pieces right side down on an ironing blanket or padded table that has been covered with a clean cloth.

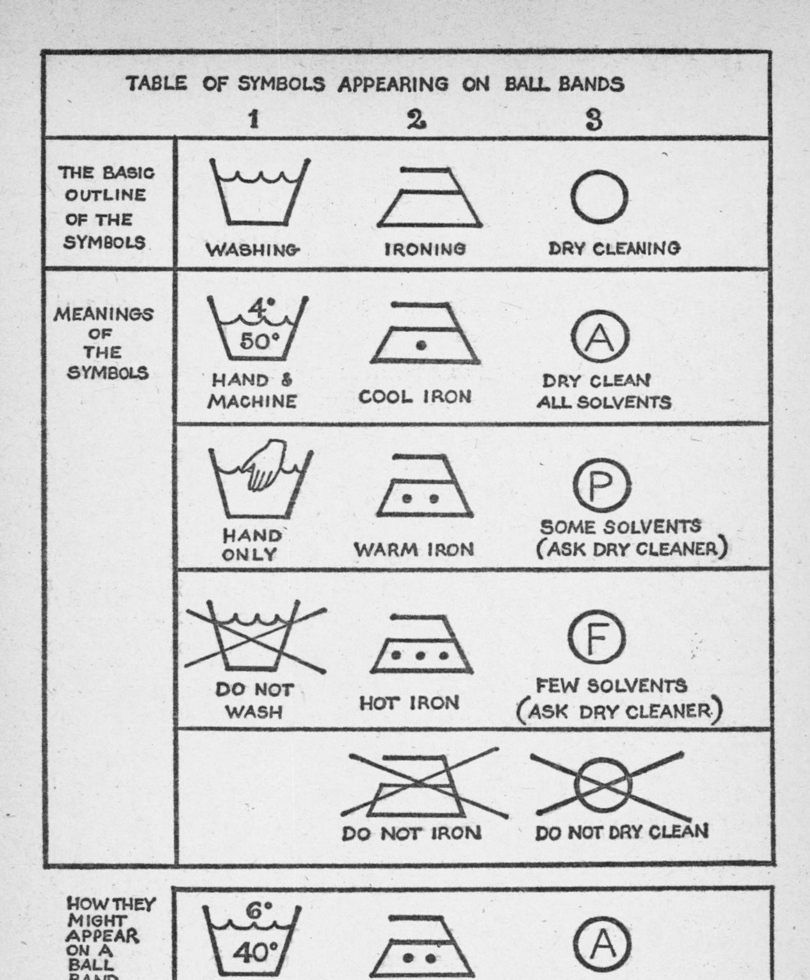

TABLE OF SYMBOLS APPEARING ON BALL BANDS

	1	2	3
THE BASIC OUTLINE OF THE SYMBOLS	WASHING	IRONING	DRY CLEANING
MEANINGS OF THE SYMBOLS	4° 50° HAND & MACHINE	COOL IRON	A DRY CLEAN ALL SOLVENTS
	HAND ONLY	WARM IRON	P SOME SOLVENTS (ASK DRY CLEANER)
	DO NOT WASH	HOT IRON	F FEW SOLVENTS (ASK DRY CLEANER)
		DO NOT IRON	DO NOT DRY CLEAN
HOW THEY MIGHT APPEAR ON A BALL BAND.	6° 40°		A

Check that the pieces have the rows running evenly across with the stitches in vertical rows. If they are at all twisted when you press them you can hardly expect them to be nice and straight afterwards.

Edges that have points or shaped motifs may need additional pinning if the most is to be made of their shaped edges.

Points should be gently pulled outwards and held in place with a pin put through into the blanket. If the pin slopes inwards very slightly it will hold upright and in place until you have finished pressing.

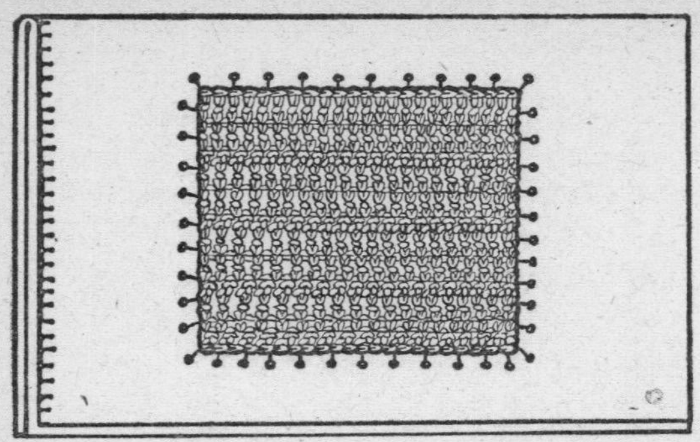

When you press wool or yarns that are made with a high percentage of wool, cover them with a clean cloth that has been wrung out in warm water and is thoroughly damp.

Place the iron over the cloth and just above it, or with the iron just touching it, so that it causes steam. Whatever you do don't move the iron about as if you were ironing a blouse or sheet or you will disturb all the stitches and push them all over the place.

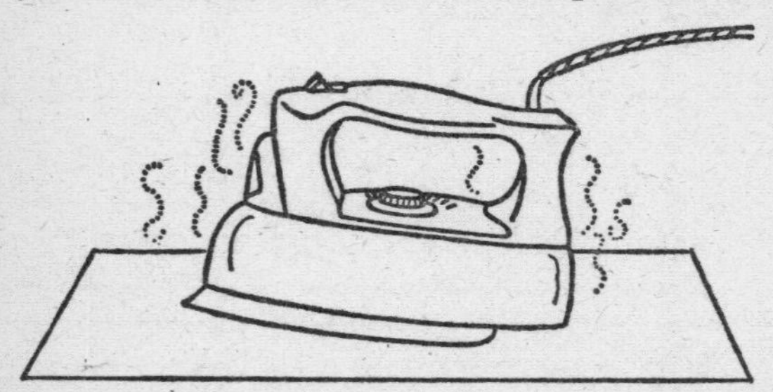

After a few seconds pick the iron up and move it to the next section until the cloth over the pieces is quite dry. Take the cloth away. Check that the crochet looks alright and that you haven't pressed in any creases that should not be there. Then remove the pins.

Although 'pressing' is always the word that we use, it creates quite the wrong impression. You do not 'press' hard on the work as the word implies for this might flatten all the nice texture of the stitches you have so carefully worked. It is the action of the hot steam through the stitches that helps to make the work become more even.

When the symbol on the ball band shows you should use a cool iron, position the pieces in just the same way but cover them with a clean dry cloth.

The cloth saves the iron from leaving a mark on the yarn and acts as a double precaution against spoiling your crochet. Perhaps you are using yarn that has no band or that has been hidden away since before bands carried these symbols. There is one way to be sure that you are right in your pressing – you can always make a tiny sample and try it out before you actually press your work.

As well as checking the ball band don't forget to check what the instructions you followed have to say. Many really chunky raised patterns may need no pressing at all, and are finished as soon as all the ends are neatly darned in place.

Seams

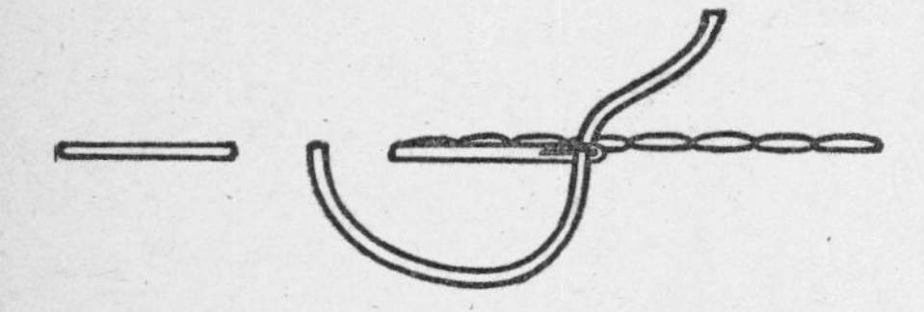

Solid work that isn't patterned or very lacy is best joined with a backstitch seam.

Place both right sides of the work together and seam along the edge on the wrong side.

Lacy pieces may be difficult to backstitch and it may be best if you use a flat woven seam, picking up a small section on one side and carrying the yarn over, picking up a small section on the other side of the work.

Don't try to rush up the edge in huge leaps with giant-sized stitches that will drag open afterwards. Rather use too many stitches but, of course, it will look best if it is just right.

Remember one thing – you already know how to crochet seams together and this may be the best way (see Chapter 8.) At least think about it. It is always quicker than sewing – but don't choose it just for speed, if you feel sewing will be better.

Yarn for seams

Unless you are using very thick yarn or an uneven, bumpy yarn the seams will look better worked in the same yarn.

However, if you crochet in a thick or uneven yarn try to get some 4 ply that is the same colour, or strand a double knitting, rather than struggling along in difficulty.

Also always use the same type of yarn. Don't seam a very thick nylon with a fine wool yarn, or the reverse, keep man-made fibres for man-made fibres and wool for wool.

Long seams

It is always time-saving to pin long seams before you sew them or crochet them together.

Pins do tend to fall out of many crochet stitches very easily so, if necessary, take time to tack along the seam. It really only takes a moment and there is nothing more annoying than sewing right to the end of a seam and finding that you really can't hide the fact that one side is considerably longer than the other, even after pulling it.

Ends that need to be darned in should always be darned into the seam rather than taken across from the seam on to the back of the actual pieces.

Zips

Zips are much easier to cope with in bags, pencil cases or garments before you do the seams.

This may seem the wrong way round but try it for yourself. Pin and tack the zip carefully to the edges that it is to join. Backstitch it securely into place.

Now join the seams and you will find that everything falls into place. This avoids the fight you can have once the 'thing' is seamed and can't be laid flat to have the zip pinned in place.

10 Patterning things

Although you may not realize it you could really manage to crochet anything you want now and could almost read any type of crochet instructions.

Just one thing we should do and that is take a look at the longer stitches.

Double trebles, triple trebles and quadruple trebles are not really 'new' stitches for they are all rather like trebles but each is a little longer than the one before. It is only made longer by having one extra stage added to it.

Double trebles (abbreviated to dtr)

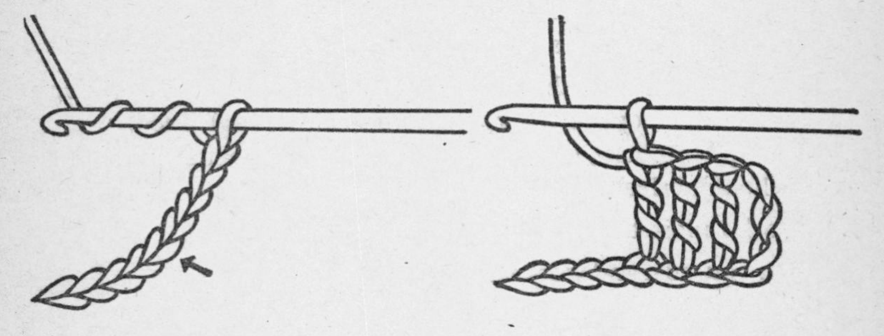

Work 16 ch.

1st row Put the yarn round the hook once and then round a second time, put the hook into the 5th ch from hook and put the yarn round the hook, then draw it back through the ch. There will be 4 loops on the hook.

Yrh and draw it through the first 2 loops (3 loops on hook), yrh and draw it through next 2 loops (2 loops on hook), yrh and draw it through the last 2 loops on the hook.
Repeat this into the 11ch left.

Did you notice how like a treble it was?

The only real difference was that you put the yarn twice round the hook at the beginning and this meant that there was one more stage to work when it came to working the loops off in pairs.

Triple trebles (abbreviated to tr tr)

This again adds one more stage to the last stitch you worked, just as the 'dtr' added one more stage to a treble.

Work 16ch.

1st row Put the yarn 3 times round the hook, put the hook into the 6th ch from the hook, yrh and draw it back through the ch. There will be 5 loops on the hook.

Now start working the loops off in pairs. Yrh and draw through first pair (4 loops on hook), yrh and draw through 2 loops (3 loops on hook), yrh and draw through the next pair (2 loops on hook), yrh and draw through the last pair.

Work 1 more tr tr in each of the next 10ch.

Can you turn and work the 2nd row?

What's more important is, can you remember how many turning chain you will need to work?

Check with Chapter 3 and you will find that it is 5 turning ch.

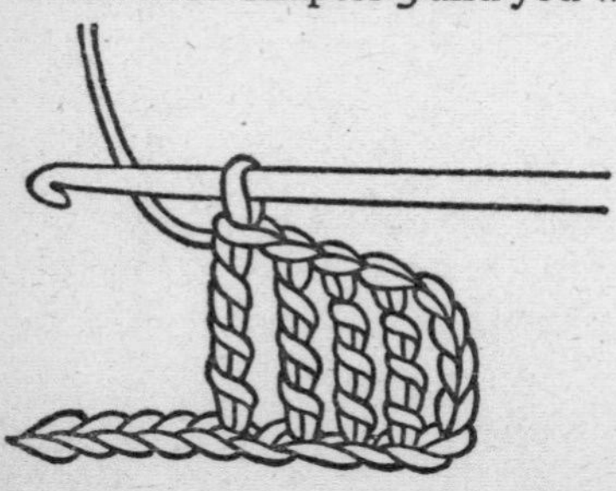

Quadruple trebles (abbreviated to quad tr)

This really is the giant of all stitches and a scarf made with it would almost be finished as soon as it was begun!

Work 16ch.

1st row Put the yarn round the hook 4 times, put the hook into the 7th ch from hook, yrh and draw it through the ch. You will have 6 loops on the hook.

Work them off as before, yrh and draw through 2 loops (5 loops on hook), yrh and draw through the next pair (4 loops on hook), yrh and draw through another 2 loops (3 loops on hook), yrh and draw through 2 loops (2 loops on hook), yrh and draw through the last pair.

Work another quad tr into each of the remaining 9ch. Turn and working 6ch for the turning ch work a 2nd row.

Double trebles are used more often than the other two although you will find all of them used in pattern-making in circles and to give variation of height.

Ridges

So far you have always worked into the top 2 threads of any stitch, but sooner or later you will come across instructions that tell you to lift 1 loop only. Which loop? The front or the back will always be mentioned because it makes quite a difference to the appearance of the stitches.

Work 12ch.

1st row Into 2nd ch from hook work 1dc, 1dc into each ch to end of row. Turn.

2nd row 1ch, * 1dc into next dc lifting back loop only, rep from * to end of row. Turn.

Repeat the 2nd row several times, taking care that you keep the same number of stitches and don't forget either to make the turning chain or to work into it.

See how ridged the result is?

Now see what happens when you work several rows of dc lifting only the front loop. It looks like another stitch altogether, doesn't it?

Chunky stitches

Stitches are sometimes made chunkier by working several times into the same stitch and then working all the loops together to complete the stitch.

There are many different ways of forming bobbles and 'popcorn' stitches as they are often called, but instructions usually tell you how to work them and they are never more difficult than the things you have already done.

One method of forming vertical ridges by placing chunky stitches on top of each other is worth trying and then you can use it to make something for yourself.

Worked in a circle it looks rather like the spokes of a wheel but it could also be used in straight lines.

Work 6ch. Join with ss to form a circle.

1st round 3ch, work 15tr into circle. Join with ss to 3rd of 3ch.

2nd round 3ch, 2tr in same st as ch, yrh and put it under the next tr bringing it out beyond the tr, yrh and draw it back round the tr, draw up the loops until they are longer than usual, about the height of the tr beside them, yrh and put the hook round the same tr again, yrh and draw up the loop, yrh, put hook round same tr, yrh and draw up the loops once more (7 loops on hook).

Yrh and draw through all the loops on hook (this is called a cluster and is abbreviated to 1cl), * 3tr in next tr, 1cl round next tr, rep from * 6 times more. Join with ss to 3rd of 3ch.

3rd round 3ch, 1tr in same st as ch, 1tr in next tr, 2tr in next tr, 1cl round next st, * 2tr in next tr, 1tr in next tr, 2tr in next tr, 1cl round next st, rep from * 6 times more. Join with ss to 3rd of 3ch.

4th round 3ch, 1tr in same st, 1tr in each of next 3tr, 2tr in next tr, 1cl round next tr, * 2tr in next tr, 1tr in each of next 3 tr, 2tr in next tr, 1cl round next tr, rep from * 6 times more. Join with ss to 3rd of 3ch. Finish off.

Workbag

This is something you will certainly need for yourself by now but which would also be an ideal gift for a friend, perhaps along with a copy of this book so that she too can learn to have fun crocheting things.

The bag is worked in the stitch you tried out in Chapter 10 and, worked in Capstan, a thick yarn, it does not take very long to make, especially as worked in the round there is no making up when it is finished.

Materials
3 (50-g) balls of Patons Capstan
1 crochet hook size 6.00

Measurements
28 cm wide by 30 cm deep

Tension
One pattern repeat measures 7 cm

To make the workbag
Begin at the top.

Work 70ch. Join with ss to form a circle.

1st round 1ch, 1dc in each ch to end. Join with ss in first ch. (70 sts)

2nd round 1ch, 1dc in each st to end. Join with a ss in first ch.

3rd round 4ch, miss 1dc, * 1tr in next dc, 1ch, miss 1dc, rep from * to end. Join with ss in 3rd of 4ch.

4th round 3ch, 1tr in 1ch sp, * 1tr in tr, 1tr in 1ch, sp, rep from * to end. Join with ss in 3rd of 3ch.

5th round 3ch, 1tr in each of next 2tr, yrh, place hook under and through next st from right to left, yrh, draw loop through and pull it up to length of trebles at side, yrh, insert hook round same st, yrh, draw it through and up, yrh, insert hook round same st, yrh, draw it through and pull it up, yrh and draw through all loops on hook, yrh, and draw it through single loop (this will be called cluster and abbreviated to cl), 1tr in each of next 3tr, * 1tr in each of next 3tr, 1cl round next st, 1tr in each of next 3tr, rep from * to end. Join with ss in 3rd of 3ch.

Rep 5th round until work measures 30 cm from edge.

Last row Turn work so that ridged side is inside tube, fold in half and seam along the bottom edge by working 1dc in each st through front and back of bag together.

Work 2 chains each 60 cm long. Thread through slotting holes at top of bag and join ends of each ch to form circles.

Darn in all ends.

11 Interesting things

The more you learn about crochet the more you will realize all its fascinating possibilities. Always there will be something new to try – new combinations of stitches or new effects of colours to experiment with.

Not only are there all these but there are many small ideas that let you add your own personal touch to quite simple crochet things like bags and pictures.

How many different flower shapes can you draw?

You could make them all in crochet: daisies, roses, carnations, and even chrysanthemums.

Roses

Work 6ch. Join with ss.

1st round 6ch, * into centre work (1tr, 3ch) 7 times. Join with ss to 3rd of 6ch.

2nd round Into each 3ch loop work (1dc, 1htr, 1tr, 1htr, 1dc). Join with a ss in first dc. Don't cut off the yarn if you want to turn this into a rose with 2 rows of petals.

3rd round At the back of the petal you have just finished (right at the lower edge of it) pick up 1 loop of the ch and work 1ss into it, keeping behind the petals you have worked make 4ch, separate the sts between the next 2 petals and work 1ss in the top of the tr that comes from the first circle up to the petals, work 4ch, ss into top of tr between petals right round the circle. Join with ss to first ss.

4th round Into each 4ch loop work (1dc, 1htr, 1tr, 1dtr, 1tr, 1htr, 1dc). Join with ss to first dc. Cut the yarn and finish off.

Try another rose working the 1st and 2nd rounds in different colours. Use the same colours for 2nd and 3rd rounds and then a different colour for the last round.

Want to experiment further?

You can go on adding rows of loops and then rows of petals until you have more rows than just 2, provided you work extra chain in the loops in each round and then also extra stitches in the petals. You can even go one stage further and work every round of petals a different shade so that you have a lovely three-dimensional flower.

But there are lots more flowers to make as well.

Dahlias

Work 8ch. Join with ss to form a circle.

1st round 4ch, work 2dtr into circle leaving last stage of each dtr on hook, yrh and draw through all 3 loops at once, 5ch, * 3dtr in circle leaving last loop of each on hook, yrh and draw through all 4 loops (cluster made), 5ch, rep from * 4 times more. Join with ss to top of first cluster. Finish off.

Chrysanthemum

Work 8ch. Join with ss to form a circle.

1st round 10ch,* into circle work (1dc, 10ch) 11 times. Join with ss to first ch. Finish off.

Daisy

Work 8ch. Join with ss to form a circle.

1st round 7ch, * into circle work (1tr, 4ch) 5 times. Join with ss to 3rd of 7ch.

2nd round Into each 4ch sp work (1dc, 1htr, 1tr, 1dtr, 1tr tr, 1dtr, 1tr, 1htr, 1dc). Join with ss in first dc. Finish off.

Why not try to invent shapes for other flowers yourself? There are a lot of different ways you can work the centres if you think about it.

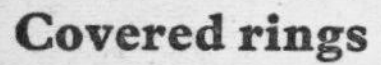

Covered rings

Woolshops sell wooden and plastic rings which can be covered with crochet and used to add to pictures, to group together to form trims for a shoulder bag or to make an interesting belt.

Even if you have difficulty in getting these rings you can try an ironmonger for rustproof metal ones or you can make a padded ring using several strands of yarn wound round your finger, round the end of a pencil or for larger rings wound round a ruler or strip of cardboard.

Once enough strands of yarn have been wound round, slip them off without cutting the yarn and crochet round the strands in double crochet just as you would do round a wooden or plastic ring.

Crocheting round a ring

Put the hook through the ring and draw through a loop of yarn taking it up to the top of the ring. Put the yarn round the hook and draw it through both the loops on the hook just as you would for double crochet.

Continue working round the ring until it is completely covered. Join the last stitch to the first with ss and finish off the yarn.

Soft rings made round a ruler and covered with crochet would make a fun fringe if after working the slip stitch you worked a few chain stitches. Work several rings like this and give each a different length of chain.

Now group them together in a cluster and sew them to the front of a crochet bag, or along the lower edge so that they dance as you walk along.

Shoulder bag

This bag is quite successful without any decoration but you can give it a distinguished look by adding the trim of covered rings we suggest.

There are lots of other trims you could add, like the flowers in this chapter, a large tassel at the point and other tassels on the flap above, or added lines of chain crochet in contrasting colours.

Materials

3 (25-g) balls of Patons Double Knitting in main colour
1 (25-g) ball of Patons Double Knitting in contrasting colour
1 crochet hook size 4.50

Three rings

Measurements

24 cm deep

Tension

8tr to 5cm

To work the shoulder bag

Begin with flap

Using main shade work 3ch.

1st row Into 3rd ch from hook work 2tr. Turn. (3sts)

2nd row 3ch, 1tr in same st, 2tr in next tr, 1tr in turning ch. Turn.

3rd row 3ch, 1tr in same st, 1tr in each of next 2tr, 2tr in next tr, 1tr in turning ch. Turn.

4th row 3ch, 1tr in same st, 1tr in each tr until 2sts remain, 2tr in next tr, 1tr in turning ch. Turn.

Rep 4th row until there are 37tr (including turning ch) in row.

Next row 3ch, 1tr in each tr to end, 1tr in turning ch. Turn.

Rep last row until straight section measures 48 cm deep. Finish off.

Fold straight section in half, wrong sides touching, and using contrast colour work 1 row dc down 1 side through both thicknesses to act as seam, along lower edge working into each st, and up other side through both thicknesses. Continue round both sides of flap and finish off.

Using contrast colour, cover rings with dc (see earlier in this chapter) and sew these on flap.

For strap cut 12 lengths of contrast and 6 lengths of the main colour of yarn each 75 cm long. Knot one end and divide the strands into 3 groups of 6 strands – 2 groups of contrast and 1 group of main colour. Plait together firmly and knot other end. Trim ends and sew to either side of bag.

You could line this bag with felt or material to give it greater strength.

12 Things galore

Now you have learned quite enough to go ahead and make any of these designs: a belt threaded with a contrasting trim; a tie that will please its wearer; a cushion or bedspread for yourself; mittens or a bonnet for a new baby, or even a clown. In this last chapter we are giving you instructions for toys, things for baby, the house, presents – and yourself. In fact, things galore.

Barbapapa

Barbapapa is worked entirely in half trebles and all that you need to know is how to increase and how to decrease.

Materials

2 (25-g) balls of Patons Trident Double Knitting
or 2 (25-g) balls of Patons Double Knitting
1 crochet hook size 4.50
Kapok or foam for stuffing
Scraps of white and black felt for eyes
Small piece of black wool for eyebrows, nose and mouth

Measurements

About 23 cm high

To work Barbapapa

Body and head

Make 4ch. Join with ss to form a circle.

1st round 1ch, 9dc into circle. Join with ss to 1ch.

2nd round 2ch, 2htr in next st, * 1htr in next st, 2htr in next st, rep from * 3 times more. Join with ss to 2nd of 2ch. (15 sts)

3rd round 2ch, * 2htr in next st, 1htr in next st, rep from * to end of round. Join with ss to 2nd of 2ch. (22 sts)

4th round 2ch, * 2htr in next st, 1htr in each of next 2 sts, rep from * to end of round. Join with ss to 2nd of 2ch. (29 sts)

5th round 2ch, 1htr in each st to end. Join with ss to 2nd of 2ch.

6–13th round Work as given for 5th round (each round will have 29 sts).

14th round 2ch, 1htr in each of next 3 sts, * 2htr in next st, 1htr in each of next 4 sts, rep from * to end of round. Join with ss to 2nd of 2ch. (34 sts)

15th and 16th rounds Work as given for 5th round. (34 sts)

17th round 2ch, 1htr in each of next 3 sts, * 2htr in next st, 1htr in each of next 4 sts, rep from * to end of round. Join with ss to 2nd of 2ch. (40 sts)

18th and 19th rounds Work as given for 5th round. (40 sts)

20th round 2ch, 1htr in each of next 3 sts, * 2htr in next st, 1htr in each of next 5sts, rep from * to end of round. Join with ss to 2nd of 2ch. (46 sts)

21st round Work as given for 5th round. (46 sts)

22nd round 2ch, 1htr in next st, * 2htr in next st, 1htr in each of next 3sts, rep from * to end of round. Join with a ss to 2nd of 2ch. (57 sts)

23rd–31st round Work as given for 5th round. (57 sts)

32nd round 2ch, 1htr in next st, * dec in next 2 sts, 1htr in each of next 3 sts, rep from * to end of round. Join with ss to 2nd of 2ch. (46 sts)

33rd round Work as given for 5th round. (46 sts)

34th round 2ch, 1htr in next st, * dec in next 2 sts, 1htr in each of next 2 sts, rep from * to end of round. Join with ss to 2nd of 2ch. (35 sts)

35th round Work as given for 5th round. (35 sts)

36th round 2ch 1htr in next st, * dec in next 2 sts, 1htr in next st, rep from * to end of round. Join with ss to 2nd of 2ch. (24 sts)

37th round Work as given for 5th round. (24 sts).

Stuff before working the last round.

Last round 2ch, 1htr in next st, * dec in next 2 sts, rep from * to end of round. Cut yarn leaving a 20-cm tail of yarn.

Thread the yarn into a wool needle and weave it around the edge of the last row. Draw it up to close the opening and darn in the ends.

Hands

Work 2 hands alike.

Make 8ch. Turn.

1st row Into 3rd ch from hook work 1htr, 1htr in each of next 5ch. Turn.

2nd row 2ch, 1htr in each of next 5 sts, 1htr in turning ch. Turn.

3rd and 4th rows Work as given for 2nd row. Cut yarn and finish off. Fold hands in half and seam, adding a little stuffing as you work the seam. Sew to either side of the body section.

Eyes, mouth and nose

Cut two ovals of white felt and sew in place for eyes. Sew 2 small black circles on the white ovals.

With black wool sew stitches in the shape of his mouth and nose. Using a crochet hook loop some short ends of black wool above his eyes, just as you would for a fringe, then trim them neatly for his eyebrows.

Clown

Quite a simple design can be turned into a delightful mascot with just one or two additions. The base of this clown is just the ball that you worked at the end of Chapter 7 and instructions are given for a small ball for his head.

Materials

1 (25-g) ball of Patons Trident Double Knitting in each of 4 colours: white, yellow, pink and black
1 crochet hook size 4.50
Stuffing
Small pieces of red wool for mouth and nose

Measurements
About 16 cm high when complete

To work the clown

Body
Using yellow make a ball as given at the end of Chapter 7. Stuff and finish off.

Arms
Work two arms alike.

Using yellow work 10ch.

1st row Into 4th ch from hook work 1tr, 1tr in each ch to end. Turn. (8 sts)

2nd row 3ch, 1tr in each of next 6 sts, 1tr in top of turning ch. Turn.

Work 2nd row 3 times more joining in white on last st.

Work 2 rows in white. Finish off.

Fold arms in half lengthways, stuff lightly as you seam them round the white hand and up the yellow sleeve. Sew one to either side of the body.

Head
Using white work 4ch. Join with a ss to form a circle.

1st round 2ch, work 15 htr into circle. Join with ss. (16 sts)

2nd round 2ch, 1htr in next st, * 2htr in next st, 1htr in next st, rep from * to end of round. Join with ss. (23 sts)

3rd round 2ch, 1htr in next st, * 2htr in next st, 1htr in each of next 2 sts, rep from * to end of round. Join with ss. (30 sts)

4th round 2ch, 1htr in each st to end. Join with ss.

5th–10th round Work as given for 4th round.

11th round 2ch, 1htr in next st, *dec in next 2 sts, 1htr in each of next 2 sts, rep from * to end. Join with ss.

12th round 2ch, 1htr in next st, * dec in next 2 sts, 1htr in next st, rep from * to end of round. Join with ss.
Stuff the head before working the last round.

Last round 2ch, 1htr in each st to end of round. Finish off leaving an end of yarn. Thread this end into a wool needle, draw up the last round and sew the head on to the top of the body, firmly.

Ruffle

Using pink work 16ch.

1st row Into 4th ch from hook work 1tr, 1tr in same st, 2tr in each ch to end. Turn.

2nd row 4ch, 2dtr in st at base of ch, 3dtr in each st to end. Finish off. Place frill round neck to form a circle and sew ends together. Sew in position.

Cuffs

Work two cuffs alike.

Using pink work 12ch.

1st row Into 5th ch from hook work 1dtr, 2dtr in same st, 3dtr in each ch to end. Finish off.

Place cuff around edge between white hand and yellow sleeve on arm and join ends to form a circle. Sew in position.

Shoes

Work two shoes alike.

Using black work 9ch.

1st row Into 3rd ch from hook work 1htr, 1htr in each ch to end. Turn.

2nd row 2ch, 1htr in each of next 6 sts, 1htr in turning ch. Turn. Rep 2nd row 5 times more. Finish off.

Fold shoes in half, stuff lightly and sew beneath body.

Face

Embroider mouth, nose and eyes with red and black wool.

Hair

Cut about 22 strips of black wool 20 cm long. Fold each strip in half and then in half again. Using the crochet hook draw the loop through the head at the side of the face. Draw the ends through the loop and pull up. Repeat all round to the other side of the face. Trim all the loops so that you have a tidy fringe forming the clown's hair.

Snowman

The snowman is made in very much the same way as the clown.

Materials

2 (25-g) balls of Patons Trident Double Knitting in white
1 (25-g) ball of Patons Trident Double Knitting in red

1 crochet hook size 4.50
Small piece of black wool for face
Stuffing

Measurements
About 16 cm high when finished

To work the snowman

Body
Using white make and stuff a ball as given at the end of Chapter 7.

Arms
Work two arms alike.

Using white only work as for the clown.

Stuff lightly and sew on to the body.

Head
Using white work a ball as given for the clown's head.
Stuff and sew securely to the body.

Scarf
Using red work 6ch.

1st row Into 4th ch from hook 1tr, 1tr in each of remaining 2ch. Turn.
2nd row 3ch, 1tr in each of next 2 sts, 1tr in 3rd of turning ch.
Rep 2nd row until scarf measures 45 cm. Finish off.
Finish each end with a small tassel.

Hat
Using red work 32ch.

1st row Into 4th ch from hook work 1tr, 1tr in each ch to end. Turn.

2nd row 3ch, 1tr in each of next 28 sts, 1tr in 3rd of turning ch. Turn. (30 sts)

3rd row 3ch, 1tr in each of next 4 sts, * dec in next 2 sts, 1tr in each of next 3 sts, rep from * to end. Turn. (25 sts)

4th row 3ch, * dec in next 2 sts, 1tr in next st, rep from * to end. Turn. (17 sts)

5th row 3ch, 1tr in each st to end. Finish off, leaving a tail of yarn. Thread this around top pulling the stitches together, then seam down the sides.

Make a small pompon and sew to the top of the hat.
Embroider black eyes and mouth.
You could add shoes like the clowns if you like.

What other people could you make?

The two balls that you have made could be turned into several different people by only changing the colours, making different facial features, and adding aprons, scarves, hats, and so on.

Things for baby

Bonnet

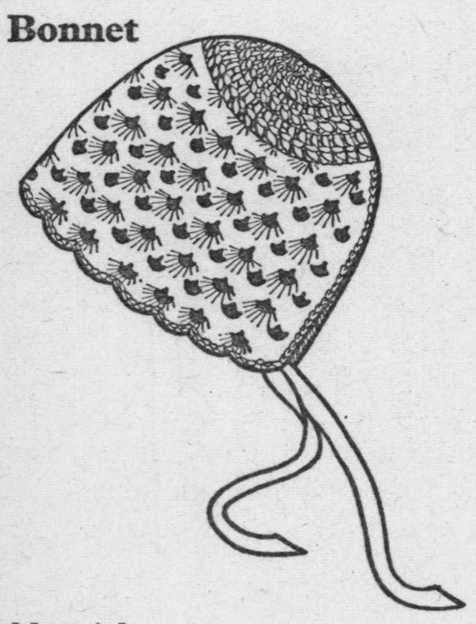

Materials
1 (25-g) ball of Patons Baby Quickerknit
1 crochet hook size 4.00
1 yard of ribbon

Measurements
To fit an average head from birth to 3 months

To work the bonnet
Work 6ch. Join with a ss to form circle.
1st round 3ch, into circle work 13tr. Join with ss to 3rd of 3ch. (14 sts)

2nd round 3ch, 1tr in same st as ss, 2tr in each st to end of round. Join with ss to 3rd of 3ch. (28 sts)

3rd round 3ch, 1tr in same st as ss, 1tr in next st, * 2tr in next st, 1tr in next st, rep from * to end of round. Join with ss to 3rd of 3ch. (42 sts)

4th round 3ch, 1tr in each of next 2 sts, * 2tr in next st, 1tr in each of next 2 sts, rep from * to end. Join with ss to 3rd of 3ch. (55 sts)

Now begin pattern which is worked in *rows* not rounds.

1st row 3ch, 1tr in next st, * miss 3 sts, in next st work (2tr, 2ch, 2tr) (this is called a group), rep from * until 5 sts are left unworked, miss 3 sts, 1tr in each of last 2 sts. Turn.

2nd row 3ch, 1tr in next st, * in 2ch sp of next group work (2tr, 2ch, 2tr), rep from * until last group has been worked into, 1tr in last tr, 1tr in top of 3ch. Turn.

Rep 2nd row 6 times more.

Last row 3ch, 1tr in next st, * into next 2ch sp work 5tr, rep from * until 2ch sp of last group has been worked into, 1tr in last tr, 1tr in top of 3ch. Do not break off the yarn. Turn and work 1 row of dc all along lower edge of bonnet.

Sew in ends.

Sew ends of ribbon to either side of lower edge.

Mittens

The same stitches may be used for many different garments and in this design the same pattern has been used as in the instructions for the baby's bonnet given previously so that you can make a matching set.

Materials

1 (25-g) ball of Patons Baby Quickerknit
1 crochet hook size 4.00
1 yard of narrow baby ribbon

Measurements

Length of mitten 12.5 cm

Tension

8htr to 5cm

To work the mittens
Work 18ch.

1st row Into 3rd ch from hook work 1htr, 1htr in each ch to end. (17 sts)

2nd row 2ch, 2htr in next st, 1htr in each of next 5 sts, 2htr in next st, 1htr in next st, 2htr in next st, 1htr in each of next 5 sts, 2htr in next st, 1htr in 2nd of turning ch. Turn. (21 sts)

3rd row 2ch, 1htr in each st to end. Turn. (21 sts)

4th row 2ch, 2htr in next st, 1htr in each of next 7 sts, 2htr in next st, 1htr in next st, 2htr in next st, 1htr in each of next 7 sts, 2htr in next st, 1htr in turning ch. Turn. (25 sts)

5th row 2ch, 1htr in each st to end. Turn.
Rep 5th row 6 times more.

Work ribbon slotting like this: 3ch, * miss next st, 1htr in next st, 1ch, rep from * to end working last htr in turning ch. Turn.

Next row * 4ch, miss 1sp, 1dc in next sp, 4ch, miss 1htr and next sp, 1dc in next st, rep from * working last dc into turning ch (8 sp). Turn.

Begin pattern for cuff.

1st row 3ch, into first sp work (1tr, 2ch, 2tr), into each of the other sp work (2tr, 2ch, 2tr). Turn.

2nd row Ss in next tr and then into first sp, 3ch, into same sp work (1tr, 2ch, 2tr), into each 2ch sp work (2tr, 2ch, 2tr). Turn.

Last row Ss in next tr and then in first sp, 3ch, into same sp work 4tr, into each 2ch sp work 5tr. Finish off.

To make up
Press lightly on wrong side under a damp cloth with a warm iron.

Seam mitten from cuff, down side, and along the top edge on the wrong side. Darn in all the ends.

Cut the ribbon in half and thread one half through the holes in the wrist of each mitten.

Pram rug

The rug is made with motifs worked alternately in pale and dark pink with each square edged in white and then white used to crochet them together on the wrong side.

Perhaps you prefer to use your own colour scheme, for example

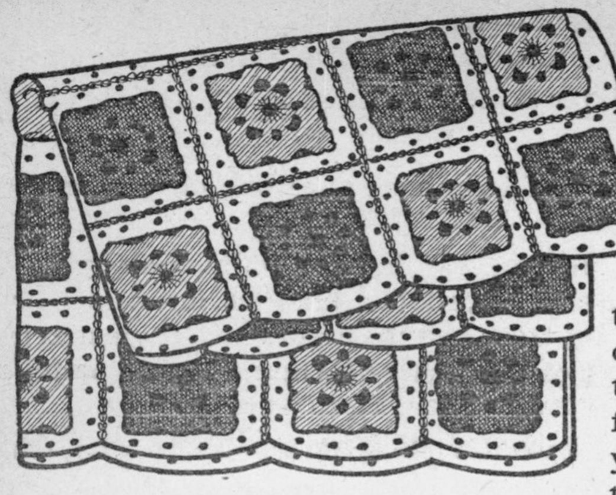

using pale and dark blue. If you alter it remember to see if it changes the quantities of yarn required. If you choose to use only two colours, one for all the motifs and one for the edging, then you will need to add the quantities of both pinks together although the white will be the same.

Should you decide to make it in one colour only, add all the quantities together.

Materials

3 (25-g) balls each of pale and dark pink Patons Trident Double Knitting
5 (25-g) balls of white Patons Trident Double Knitting
1 crochet hook size 4.50

Measurements

Each motif measures about 10 cm square
The rug was made from 35 squares, 5 squares across and 7 squares long
Finished complete size about 50 cm by 70 cm

To work the pram rug

Motif

When working motif the right side of the work is facing you.

Using pale pink work 6ch. Join with ss to form a circle.

1st round 3ch, work 15tr into circle. Join with ss in 3rd of 3ch.

2nd round 5ch, 1dc in next tr, * 5ch miss 2tr, 1dc in next tr, 4ch, 1dc in next tr, rep from * twice more, 5ch. Join with ss in first of 5ch.

3rd round Ss in first ch loop, into same loop work (2dc, 3ch, 2dc), into next 5ch loop work (1dc, 1htr, 1tr, 1ch, 1dtr, 1ch, 1tr, 1htr, 1dc), * into next 4ch loop work (2dc, 3ch, 2dc), into next 5ch loop work (1dc, 1htr, 1tr, 1ch, 1dtr, 1ch, 1tr, 1htr, 1dc) rep from * twice more, joining to first ss with ss. Cut yarn and finish off.

Work 16 more motifs in pale pink and 18 motifs in dark pink.

Edging

With right side of motif facing and using white join yarn into corner dtr on motif.

1st round 2ch, 1dc in same st as ch, * 2ch, 1dc in next tr, 3ch, 1dc in 3ch loop on side, 3ch, 1dc in next tr, 2ch, into corner dtr work (1dc, 1ch, 1dc), rep from * twice more, 2ch, 1dc in next tr, 3ch, 1dc in 3ch loop on side, 3ch, 1dc in next tr, 2ch, join with ss in first ch.

2nd round Ss into corner ch sp, 4ch, into same sp work 1tr, 1ch, 2tr in next 2ch sp, 1ch (3tr in next 3ch sp, 1ch) twice, 2tr in next 2ch sp, 1ch, * into corner ch work (1tr, 1ch, 1tr), 1ch, 2tr in next 2ch sp, 1ch, (3tr in next 3ch sp, 1ch) twice, 2tr in next 2ch sp, 1ch, rep from * twice more, joining with ss to 3rd of 4ch. Cut yarn and finish off.

To make up

Work edging round all the other motifs in the same way. Decide how you are going to arrange the motifs and then join the sides together on the wrong side using slip stitch. When all the motifs are joined along the sides into strips, place the right sides of 2 strips together and work them together using slip stitch. Join the other strips in the same way.

Finish the rug by pressing lightly on the wrong side under a damp cloth with a warm iron.

Shawl

Made in a simple lace stitch this shawl has an easy and different crochet fringe.

Materials

4 (20-g) balls of Patons Double Plus
1 crochet hook size 5.00

Measurements

About 53 cm deep at centre back

To work the shawl

Begin at centre back point.

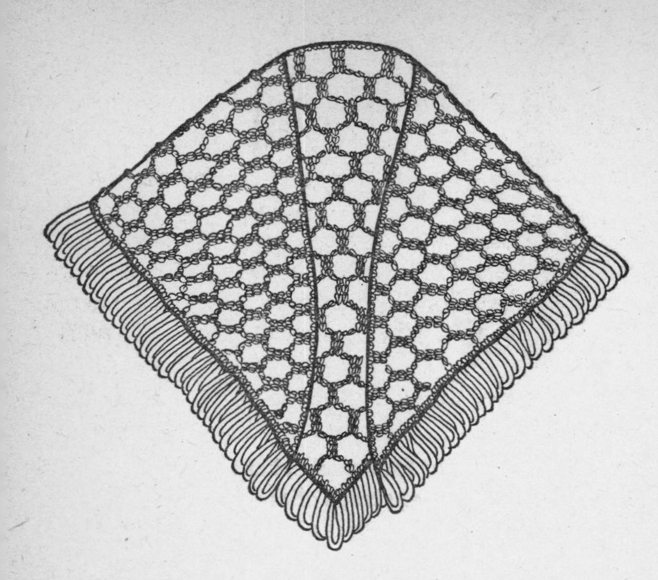

Work 6ch, without turning work 1tr into the first ch, thus forming a triangle.

1st row 6ch, into loop of triangle work (2tr, 3ch, 1tr). Turn.

2nd row 6ch, * into loop work 2tr, 3ch, rep from * once, work 1tr into last sp. Turn.
3rd row 6ch, * into next loop work 2tr, 3ch rep from * to end, completing the row by working 1tr into last loop. Turn.
Rep 3rd row until 34 rows have been worked. Finish off.

Fringe
Join yarn into first loop on short side at right-hand side of shawl, into this loop work (30ch, 1dc, 30ch, 1dc, 30ch), * into next loop work (1dc, 30ch, 1dc, 30ch), rep from * down one side and up the other, ending with 1dc in last loop, leaving the long third side plain.

To complete
Darn in all ends.

The shawl should not require any pressing.

Round kettle or pot holder

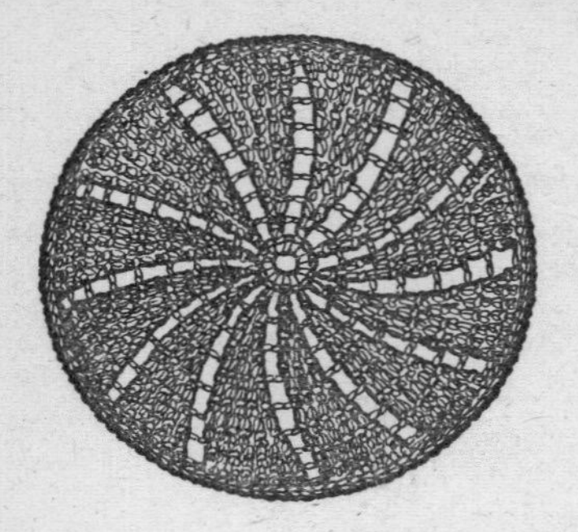

Always popular as presents or for bazaars, kettle and pot holders need not be plain, uninteresting scraps of crochet. Instructions given here are for a round one which is a little like a spider's web. It is lined to give thickness and also so that the contrast shows through the front pattern, making it attractive and colourful.

Materials
1 (25-g) ball in each of two contrasting colours of Patons Trident Double Knitting
1 crochet hook size 4.50

Measurements
About 18 cm diameter when completed

To make the round holder
When working circles the right side of the work is facing you.

Front
Using 1st colour work 6ch. Join with ss to form circle.

1st round 4ch, * 1tr into circle, 1ch, rep from * 10 times more. Join with ss to 3rd of 4ch.

2nd round 5ch, miss 1ch, * into next tr work 1tr, 2ch, miss 1ch, rep from * to end. Join with ss in 3rd of 5ch.

3rd round 3ch, 1tr in same st as ss, 3ch, * 2tr in next tr, 3ch, rep from * to end. Join with ss in 3rd of 3ch.

4th round 3ch, 2tr in next tr, 3ch, * 1 tr in next tr, 2tr in next tr, 3ch, rep from * to end. Join with ss in 3rd of 3ch.

5th round 3ch, 1tr in next tr, 2tr in next tr, 3ch, * 1tr in each of next 2tr, 2tr in next tr, 3ch, rep from * to end. Join with ss in 3rd of 3ch.

6th round 3ch, 1tr in each of next 2tr, 2tr in next tr, 3ch, * 1tr in each of next 3tr, 2tr in next tr, 3ch, rep from * to end. Join with ss in 3rd of 3ch.

7th round 3ch, 1tr in each of next 3tr, 2tr in next tr, 3ch, * 1tr in each of next 4tr, 2tr in next tr, 3ch, rep from * to end. Join as before.
Finish off.

Backing
Using 2nd colour work 4ch. Join with ss to form circle.

1st round 3ch, work 11 tr into circle. Join with ss in 3rd of 3ch.

2nd round 3ch, 1tr in same st as ss, * 2tr in next tr, rep from * to end. Join with ss to 3rd of 3ch.

3rd round 3ch, 2tr in next tr, * 1tr in next tr, 2tr in next tr, rep from * to end. Join with ss in 3rd of 3ch.

4th round 3ch, 1tr in next tr, 2tr in next tr, * 1tr in each of next 2tr, 2tr in next tr, rep from * to end. Join with ss in 3rd of 3ch.

5th round 3ch, 1tr in same st as ss, 1tr in each of next 3tr, * 2tr in next tr, 1tr in each of next 3tr, rep from * to end. Join with ss in 3rd of 3ch.

6th round 3ch, 1tr in each of next 3tr, * 2tr in next tr, 1tr in each of next 4tr, rep from * to last tr, 2tr in last tr. Join with ss in 3rd of 3ch.

7th round 3ch, 1tr in next tr, * 2tr in next tr, 1tr in each of next 5tr, rep from * to last 4 sts, 2tr in next tr, 1tr in each of next 3tr. Join with ss in 3rd of 3ch. (84 sts) Do not finish off.

Joining round Place 1st circle behind the circle you have just made, wrong sides touching, and insert the hook with the loop still on it through next st on circle you have just made and through any of the first (right-hand) tr of a treble group on 1st circle. Work 1dc through both layers, work 1dc through each of the next 5tr matching back to front, * 3ch, miss 1tr on back circle and 3ch sp on front and work 1dc in each of next 6tr through both layers, rep from * to end, finishing with 3ch. Join with ss to first st. Finish off all ends.

Cushion

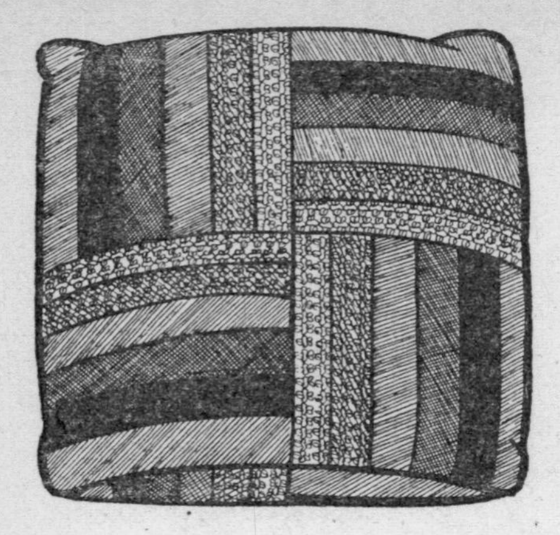

Do you remember trying out stitches that were worked into only 1 strand of the loop instead of into both loops ? If not look back at Chapter 10.

Here is a cushion which is worked in patchwork squares made in rows of double crochet worked into the back loop of the previous row only.

These squares were each worked in 6 different colours. You could work from white through grey to black, from cream to deepest chocolate, from water green through lovely minty shades to forest green or even in the rainbow colours chosen for this sample, emerald, royal blue, purple, scarlet, orange and yellow.

Materials

1 (25-g) ball of Patons Trident Double Knitting in each of 6 colours: emerald, royal blue, purple, scarlet, orange, yellow
1 crochet hook size 4.50
Cushion pad or stuffing

Measurements

Each square measures about 15 cm. The finished cushion with 4 squares back and front measures 30 cm square

To make the cushion

Make each of the eight squares as follows:
Using emerald or 1st colour work 25ch.

1st row Into 2nd ch from hook work 1dc, 1dc in each of next 23 ch. Turn.

2nd row 1ch, miss first st, 1dc in each of next 23 sts remembering to work into only the back loop of each stitch. 1dc in turning ch. Turn.

Rep 2nd row twice more working only the first half of the last stitch on the last row, Join in blue or the 2nd colour by completing the second part of the last dc.

Work 4 rows more joining in purple or 3rd colour on the last stitch of 4th row.

Work 4 rows in each of the remaining colours, joining each colour on the second part of the last stitch of the 4th row.

When all 6 colours have been worked, finish off.

Make 7 more squares like this.

To make up
Pin each square out neatly and press very lightly on wrong side under a damp cloth with a warm iron.

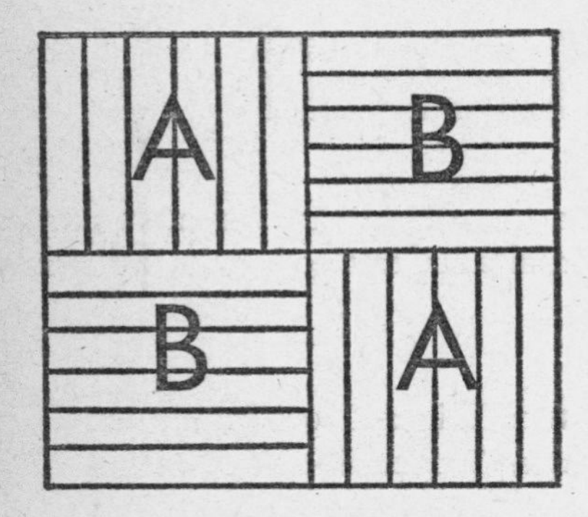

Sew the squares together, always altering the ridges on the next square so that all the squares marked A on the diagram have the ridges running up and down the square, and the squares marked B have the ridges running across.

Put front and back together and work a row of dc in 1 colour only around 3 edges through both back and front edges, and along the front edge only on the 4th side. Finish off ends.

Insert the cushion pad or stuffing and seam the remaining edge.

Table mats

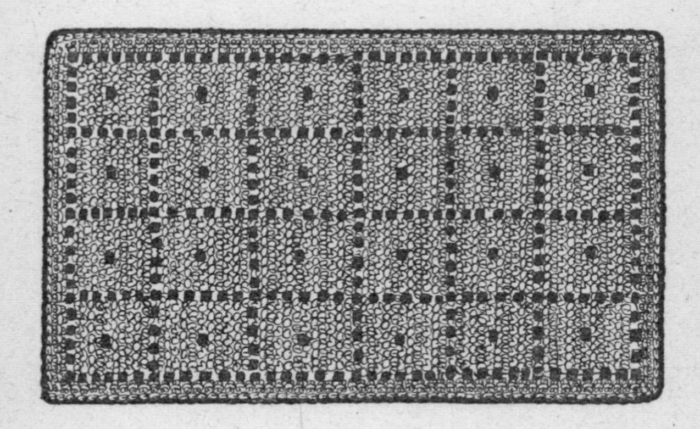

Openwork squares contrast against solid squares to make a simple design either for a small mat or for a larger place mat, worked in treble crochet.

Materials
Small mat – 1 (25-g) ball of Patons Trident Double Knitting
Place mat – 3 (25-g) balls of Patons Trident Double Knitting
1 crochet hook size 4.50

Measurements
Small mat – about 15 cm square, when complete
Place mat – about 28 cm by 42 cm, when complete

To work the table mats
For small mat work 32ch, for place mat work 56ch.

1st row Into 8th ch from hook work 1tr, 2ch, miss 2ch, * 1tr in next ch, 2ch, miss 2ch, rep from * to last ch, 1tr in last ch. Turn.

2nd row 5ch, miss first tr, * (1tr in next tr, 2tr in next sp) 3 times, 1tr in next tr, 2ch, rep from * to last sp, 1tr in 5th of 7 turning ch. Turn.

3rd row 5ch, miss first tr, * 1tr in each of next 10tr, 2ch, rep from * to last sp, 1tr in 3rd of 5 turning ch. Turn.

4th row 5ch, miss first tr, * 1tr in each of next 4tr, 2ch, miss 2tr, 1tr in each of next 4tr, 2ch, rep from * to last sp, 1tr in 3rd of 5 turning ch. Turn.

5th row 5ch, miss first tr, * 1tr in each of next 4tr, 2tr in sp, 1tr in each of next 4tr, 2ch, rep from * to last sp, 1tr in 3rd of 5 turning ch. Turn.

6th row As 3rd row.

7th row 5ch, miss first tr, * (1tr in next tr, 2ch, miss 2tr) 3 times, 1tr in next tr, 2ch, rep from * to last sp, 1tr in 3rd of 5 turning ch. Turn.

8th row Work as for 2nd row, but working last tr in 3rd of 5 turning ch. Turn. Rep 3rd to 7th row once for small mat and 3rd to 8th row 4 times, then 3rd to 7th row again for place mat.

Last row Do not turn work but work ss into corner sp, 3ch then work along first edge, 1tr in same sp, * into next sp work 2tr, rep from * to next corner, into corner sp work 2tr, 3ch, 2tr, work along each side working 2tr in each sp and (2tr, 3ch, 2tr) in next 2 corners. When the edge is complete work 2tr into last corner, 3ch and join with ss to 3rd of first 3ch.

To complete

Pin mats out carefully, keeping edges straight.

Press on the wrong side under a damp cloth with a warm iron.

Two for the pots

Using the same interesting stitch but in different stripe widths, here are two pot covers – a rectangular one for a tea pot and a tall one for a coffee pot.

Tea pot cosy

Materials

2 (25-g) balls of Patons Trident Double Knitting in each of 1st and 3rd colours, and 1 (25-g) ball in 2nd colour

1 crochet hook size 4.50

Measurements

Finished cosy about 25 cm by 20 cm high

To work the tea pot cosy

Begin at lower edge with 1st colour.

With 1st colour work 49ch.

1st row Into 3rd ch from hook work 1dc, * 1ch, miss 1ch, 1dc in next ch, rep from * to end. Turn.

2nd row 3ch, * 1 dc in next ch sp, 1ch, rep from * to end, working first part of dc into last ch sp, work 2nd part of stitch using 2nd colour. Turn.

3rd row 3ch, * 1dc in next ch sp, 1ch, rep from * to last sp, 1dc in last sp. Turn.

Work next row as for 2nd row changing colour at end of row to 3rd colour, then work as for 3rd and 2nd rows using 3rd colour, changing to 1st colour at end of last row.

Continue in this way, repeating the 3rd and 2nd rows using the colours in the same order, changing colour after every 2 rows. Continue until work measures 20cm from start. Finish off.

Work 2nd piece in same way.

Place both sections together, wrong sides touching. Join one colour to right-hand side at lower edge and work edging thus: 1dc, 1ch, * into first row of next stripe work 1dc, 1ch, rep from * to top of side edge, then along top edge work ** 1dc, 1ch, miss 1 st, rep from ** to end, now work along other side as you did the first side. Finish off.

Join the 2nd colour to the lower edge of right-hand side and work 1ch, * 1dc into next ch sp, rep from * along side, top and other side ending 1dc in last st. Finish off.

Darn in all ends.

Coffee pot cosy

Materials
2 (25-g) balls in each of 3 colours of Patons Trident Double Knitting
1 crochet hook size 4.50

Measurements
About 21 cm high and 50 cm round

To work the coffee pot cosy
The cosy is worked in 4 sections. If you find that your pot has a spout or handle that juts out quite a lot you may find that the cosy will fit better if you leave part of 2 of the seams open so that the spout and handle can have more room.

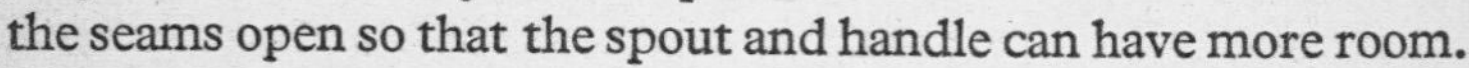

Begin at lower edge.

Using 1st colour work 25ch.

1st row Into 3rd ch from hook work 1dc, 1ch, miss 1ch, * 1dc in next ch, 1ch, miss 1ch, rep from * ending with 1dc in last ch. Turn.

2nd row 3ch, * 1dc in next ch sp, 1ch, rep from * ending with 1dc in last sp. Turn.

Rep 2nd row twice more joining in 2nd colour on last st.

Continue in this way working 2nd row but joining in next colour at end of every 4th row, until work measures 18cm.

Keeping stripe sequence correct dec at each end of every row as follows: *Dec row* ss in first dc and into first ch sp, 3ch, * 1dc in next sp, 1ch, rep from * until 2 sp rem, 1dc in next sp. Turn.

Rep this row 4 times more. Finish off.

Seam the 4 pieces on the wrong side or crochet together as given for the tea cosy, joining the corners of each dec row and leaving the very centre open.

Trim

Using any colour work 10ch. Join with ss to form circle.

1st row * 12 ch, 1dc in circle, rep from * 9 times more. Join with ss to first ch.

Finish off.

Make one circle of each colour in this way.

Sew one inside the other and then all three to top of cosy.

Things for presents – and yourself!

Pencil case

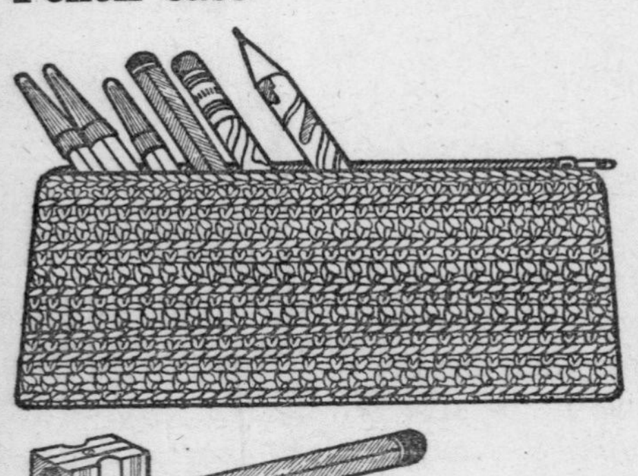

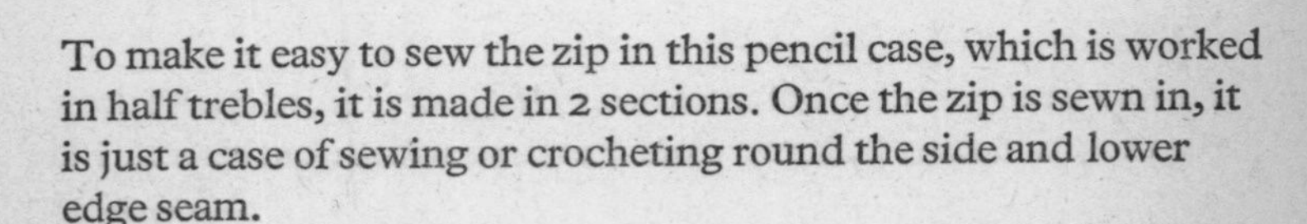

To make it easy to sew the zip in this pencil case, which is worked in half trebles, it is made in 2 sections. Once the zip is sewn in, it is just a case of sewing or crocheting round the side and lower edge seam.

Materials

1 (25-g) ball of Patons Trident Double Knitting

1 crochet hook size 4.50

1 zip 20 cm long

Measurements
20 cms long and 8 cm deep

Tension
8htr to 5 cm

To work the pencil case
Two pieces, which are exactly the same, are made for the front and the back as follows:

Work 36ch.

1st row Into 3rd ch from hook work 1htr, 1htr in each of next 33 ch. Turn. (35 sts)

2nd row 2ch, 1htr in each of next 33 htr, 1htr in turning ch. Turn.

Rep 2nd row until section measures 8 cm. Finish off.

Make 2nd piece in exactly the same way.

To make up
Lay zip flat, wrong side up, and place one section, also wrong side up, along the zip with the edge immediately below or under the zip tape, one on either side.

Pin and tack very carefully in place.

Backstitch securely in place.

With right sides of case touching, seam around sides and lower edge before turning right side out.

Spectacle case

One for her and one for him gives you the chance to make something very simple in double crochet and also to try out a very pretty shell stitch which is not nearly as difficult as it looks and consists only of trebles and double crochet.

Her case

Materials
1 (25-g) ball of Patons Trident Double Knitting
1 crocket hook size 4.50

Measurements
Finished case measures 7.5 cm by 16 cm

To make her case
Begin at lower edge by working 16ch.

1st row Into 4th ch from hook work 1tr, 1tr in same st, miss 2ch, 1dc in next ch, miss 2ch, 5tr in next ch (this is called a group), miss 2ch, 1dc in next ch, miss 2ch, 3tr in last ch. Turn.

2nd row 1ch, 5tr in first dc, 1dc in centre of 5tr group, 5tr in next dc, 1dc in top of turning ch. Turn.

3rd row 3ch, 2tr in first dc, 1dc in centre of next 5tr group, 5tr in next dc, 1dc in centre of 5tr group, 3tr in turning ch. Turn.

Rep 2nd and 3rd rows 7 times more. Finish off.

Work 2nd piece in the same way.

Place both pieces together and join both side seams and lower edge seam.

His case

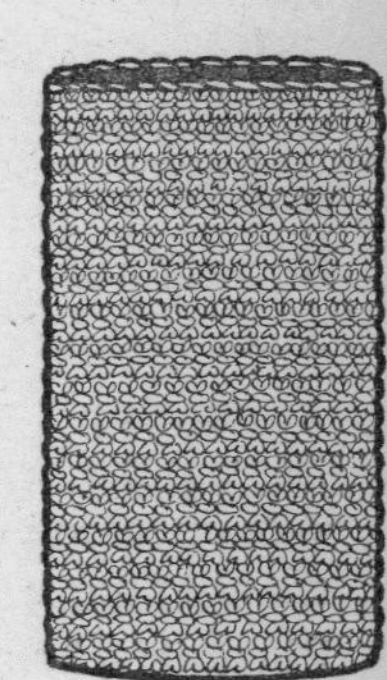

Materials

1 (25-g) ball of Patrons Trident Double Knitting

1 crochet hook size 4.50

Measurements

About same size as her case

To make his case.

Work 17ch.

1st row Into 2nd ch from hook work 1dc, 1dc in each ch to end. Turn.

2nd row 1ch, miss first st, working into front loop only. 1dc in each st to end, 1dc in turning ch. Turn.

Rep 2nd row throughout until strip measures 36 cm long. Finish off.
Fold in half and seam along sides on wrong side or crochet side seams together with dc on right side.

Cap

Chunky crochet makes a super cap to team with the scarf that follows in a matching pattern. The cap is topped by a crocheted version of a pompon.

Materials

1 (50-g) ball of Patons Capstan

1 crochet hook size 6.00

Measurements

To fit average 8- to 14-year-old head

To work the cap

Begin at the centre top.

Work 6ch. Join with ss to form a circle.

1st round 3ch, work 15tr into circle. Join with ss to 3rd of 3ch.

2nd round 4ch, 1tr in same st as ss, * 1tr in next st, in next st work (1tr, 1ch, 1tr), rep from * to last st, 1tr in last st. Join with ss to 3rd of 4ch.

3rd round Ss in first sp, 3ch, in same sp work (1tr, 1ch, 2tr), * miss 3 sts, in next sp work (2tr, 1ch, 2tr), rep from * to end. Join with ss in 3rd of 3ch.

4th round Ss in next st and next sp, 3ch, in same sp work (1tr, 2ch, 2tr), * in next 1ch sp work (2tr, 2ch, 2tr) (this is a group), rep from * to end. Join with ss in 3rd of 3ch.

5th round Ss in next st and next sp, 3ch, in same sp work (1tr, 2ch, 2tr), * 1tr in sp before next group, into next 2ch sp work (2tr, 2ch, 2tr), rep from * ending 1tr in sp before next group. Join with ss in 3rd of 3ch.

6th round Ss in next st and next sp, 3ch, into same sp work (1tr, 2ch, 2tr), * miss 2tr, 2tr in next tr, into next 2ch sp work (2tr, 2ch, 2tr), rep from * ending miss 2tr, 2tr in next tr. Join with ss in 3rd of 3ch.

7th round Ss in next st and next sp, 3ch, into same sp work (1tr, 2ch, 2tr), * miss 2tr, 1tr in each of next 2tr, into next 2ch sp work (2tr, 2ch, 2tr), rep from * ending miss 2tr, 1tr in each of next 2tr to end. Join with ss in 3rd of 3ch.

Rep 7th round 3 times more. Finish off.

Trimming
Work 6ch. Join with ss to form a circle.

1st round * 14ch, 1dc into circle, rep from * 17 times more. Join with ss to first ch. Finish off ends and sew to centre top of cap.

Scarf

This chunky stitch does not take very long to crochet and will make you a lovely warm scarf.

Materials
3 (50-g) balls of Patons Capstan
1 crochet hook size 6.00

Measurements
140 cm long

Tension
One pattern repeat measures about 6 cm

To work scarf

Start at centre back by working 25ch.

1st row 1 tr in 4th ch from hook, 1tr in next ch, * miss 3ch, in next ch work (2tr, 2ch, 2tr) (this is a group), miss 3ch, 1tr in each of next 3 ch, rep from * to end. Turn.

2nd row 3ch, 1tr in each of next 2tr, * in 2ch sp work (2tr, 2ch, 2tr), miss 2 tr of group, 1tr in each of next 3tr, rep from * to end. Turn.

Rep 2nd row until work measures 70 cm or half the required finished length.

Finish off.

Now work into the loops left from the starting ch at centre back. Rejoin yarn to first loop, 3ch, 1tr in each of next 2 loops, * into loop below next group work (2tr, 2ch, 2tr), 1tr in loop below each of next 3tr, rep from * to end.

Rep 2nd row as for other side until the 2nd side is the same length as the first. Finish off.

To complete
Darn in all ends and press lightly on the wrong side under a damp cloth with a warm iron.

Belt

This belt can be made to match your play clothes or wear with something very special, just as you like.
Worked in treble crochet it is threaded with chains of contrasting colour and tied with the same colour.

Materials

1 (25-g) ball of Patons Trident Double Knitting in the main shade
1 (25-g) ball of Patons Trident Double Knitting in contrasting colour for trim and ties
1 crochet hook size 4.50

To work the belt

Work 10ch using the main shade.

1st row Into 4th ch from hook work 1tr, * 1ch, miss 1ch, 1tr in each of next 2 ch, rep from * once more. Turn.

2nd row 3ch, 1tr in next tr, * 1ch, 1tr in each of next 2tr, rep from * once more, working last tr in top of 3ch.
Repeat 2nd row until the belt is the required length. Finish off and darn in the ends.

Trim

Using contrast, work 2 long chains about 10 cm longer than the finished belt. Thread each chain through the row of holes, sewing the ends in place at the back.

Work a 3rd chain about 40 cm longer, thread through the top edges at either side of the front, cross and thread through the lower edges to act as the tie.

Nightdress case

A circular nightdress case is very easy to make in chains and trebles. It can look very dainty and far more intricate than it really is if you decorate it with roses or the other flower motifs shown in Chapter 11.

Materials

4 (25-g) balls of Patons Trident Double Knitting in white
1 (25-g) ball each of Patons Trident Double Knitting in pale pink and dark pink for roses
1 crochet hook size 4.50

Measurements

Across finished circle about 32 cm

To work the nightdress case

Front

Work 6ch. Join with ss to form circle.

1st round 4ch, * 1tr into circle, 1ch, rep from * 10 times more. Join with ss to 3rd of first 4ch.

2nd round Ss into next sp, 3ch, 1tr in same sp, 2ch, * 2tr in next sp, 2ch, rep from * to end. Join with ss to 3rd of 3ch.

3rd round Ss in next st, then into next sp, 3ch, 1tr in same sp, 3ch, * 2tr in next sp, 3ch, rep from * to end. Join with ss to 3rd of 3ch.

4th round Ss in next st, then in next sp, 3ch, 2tr in same sp, 3ch, * 3tr in next sp, 3ch, rep from * to end. Join with ss in 3rd of 3ch.

5th round Ss in next 2 sts and then in next sp, 3ch 2tr in same sp, 4ch, * 3tr in next sp, 4ch, rep from * to end. Join with ss to 3rd of [illegible]ch.

[illegible] 4ch, miss 1tr, 1tr in next st, 1ch, into next sp work (1tr, [illegible]ch, * 1tr in next tr, 1ch, miss 1tr, 1tr in next tr, 1ch, [illegible] work (1tr, 1ch, 1tr), 1ch, rep from * to end. Join [illegible]rd of 4ch.

7th round 3ch, 1tr in next sp, * 1tr in next st, 1tr in next sp, rep from * to end. Join with ss in 3rd of 3ch.

8th round 3ch, 1tr in next st, 2ch, miss 1tr, * 1tr in each of next 2 sts, 2ch, miss 1tr, rep from * to end. Join with ss in 3rd of 3ch.

9th round Ss in next st and then in next sp, 3ch, 1tr in same sp, 3ch, * into next sp work 2tr, 3ch, rep from * to end. Join with ss in 3rd of 3ch.

10th round Ss in next st and then into sp, 3ch, 2tr in same sp, 3ch, * into next sp work 3tr, 3ch, rep from * to end. Join with ss in 3rd of 3ch.

11th round 3ch, 1tr in each of next 2 sts, 2tr in next sp, * 1tr in each of next 3 sts, 2tr in next sp, rep from * to end. Join with ss in 3rd of 3ch.

12th round 6ch, miss 4tr, * 1dc in next st, 5ch, miss 4 tr, rep from * to end. Join with ss in first of 6ch.

13th round Into first loop work (1dc, 1htr, 2tr, 1htr, 1dc), * 1ss in dc between loops, into next loop work (1dc, 1htr, 2tr, 1htr, 1dc), rep from * to end. Join with ss into first dc. Finish off.

Back

Work as given for the front until the 11th round has been completed. Finish off.

Roses

Work 3 roses as given in Chapter 11, working the first round in white, 2nd and 3rd rounds in pale pink and the 4th round in dark pink.

Darn in the ends.

Press both circles lightly under a damp cloth with a warm iron on the wrong sides.

Sew roses to centre of front.

Join back and front edges along half of 11th round leaving a large opening.

Tie

This plain tie makes a perfect gift for the man in your life, whether he is father, uncle, cousin, godfather, or even your older brother. It is worked completely in half trebles and so does not take very long to make.

Materials

2 (25-g) balls of Patons Trident Double Knitting
1 crochet hook size 4.50

Measurements

130 cm long and about 7 cm across at widest part

Tension

8 htr to 5 cm

To work the tie

Begin with narrowest part.

Work 7ch.

1st row Into 3rd ch from hook work 1htr, 1htr in each of next 4ch. Turn.

2nd row 2ch, miss first st, 1htr in each of next 4sts, 1htr in turning ch. Turn. (6 sts) Rep 2nd row until tie measures 70 cm.
Start shaping.

1st row 2ch, miss first st, inc by working 2htr in next st, 1htr in each of next 2 sts, 2htr in next st, 1htr in turning ch. Turn. (8 sts)

2nd row 2ch, miss first st, 1htr in each st, 1htr in turning ch. Turn. Rep 2nd row 10 times more.

3rd row 2ch, miss first st, inc by working 2htr in next st, 1htr in each of next 4 sts, 2htr in next st, 1htr in turning ch. Turn. (10 sts)

4th row 2ch, miss first st, 1htr in each st, 1htr in turning ch. Turn. Rep last row 10 times more.

5th row 2ch, miss first st, inc by working 2htr in next st, 1htr in each of next 6 sts, 2htr in next st, 1htr in turning ch. Turn. (12 sts)

6th row 2ch, miss first st, 1htr in each st, 1htr in turning ch. Turn. Rep last row until work measures 130 cm. Finish off.

To complete

Darn in ends and press lightly on the wrong side under a damp cloth with a warm iron.